P9-BYD-683

PRAISE FOR *YOUR HIDDEN SUPERPOWER*

"Adrienne is right . . . the secret to success lies in relationships. The greatest relationships are created by a want and/or a need to partner with someone else. Getting to work with someone who is kind, thoughtful, and has your back as a partner is what we all want. Kindness is vastly under measured, yet it lies as that foundation to the best partnerships . . . personally and professionally."

—Garth Brooks

"I loved being interviewed on TV by the warm and perceptive Adrienne Bankert. I could have talked to her all day. Her empathy and humanity were a delight. In her book, she explains her philosophy on life, work, and connections in a relatable and easy-to-read way. I hope it will spread the word kindness to a wider, waiting world."

—Anthony Daniels, Actor, Author,
I Am C-3PO: The Inside Story

"Adrienne is a magical soul . . . she never ceases to amaze me with her unique ability to meet someone and, in minutes, find a way to emotionally and energetically meet you exactly where you are. I've witnessed it time and time again, but when she points her superpower at you, it stirs your soul and awakens empathy muscles that I think we forget as adults. I call her my Kindness Guru because no matter how complex and convoluted the challenge I bring to her, she inspires answers that make your spirit feel good, and this book is a testament to that spirit."

—Omar Johnson, Former VP of Marketing, Apple

YOUR HIDDEN SUPERPOWER

YOUR HIDDEN SUPERPOWER

THE KINDNESS THAT MAKES YOU UNBEATABLE AT WORK AND CONNECTS YOU WITH ANYONE

ADRIENNE BANKERT

HarperCollins Leadership

An Imprint of HarperCollins

Published by HarperCollins Leadership, an imprint of HarperCollins Focus LLC.

ISBN 978-1-4002-1820-2 (eBook)
ISBN 978-1-4002-1814-1 (HC)

Library of Congress Cataloging-in-Publication Data

Library of Congress Cataloging-in-Publication application has been submitted.

Printed in the United States of America

20 21 22 23 LSC 10 9 8 7 6 5 4 3 2 1

I dedicate this book to everyone who wants to have it all. May we live "all in" with our relationships, dreams, and identity. To the world changers, mountain movers, and breakthrough agents, let's agree to live authentically and wholeheartedly with kindness. When we know who we truly are, nothing can stop us.

CONTENTS

FOREWORD

Kindness has become too rare of a commodity.

Some things are more precious than gold. Time is one of them and kindness, in the midst of our priceless hours and minutes, is another. Whether with loved ones or with those we cross paths with in our daily lives, kindness is given and received in an exchange that helps us to truly enjoy the world around us. Every person, at one time or another, would benefit greatly from kindness.

Investing what seems like a mere moment can have a tremendous impact. Making time to care for someone we didn't previously know helps us snap out of going through the motions and realize that we're dealing with *real people.* From the hotel housekeeper to the top executive having lunch, they each have gifts, needs, and stories to share that we can become a part of. Being kind to the busser at every restaurant I dine in communicates how important that person is to my experience, which in turn flows to my food server and the cook. The way we treat one person has a ripple effect on each consecutive person we come in contact with. Also, how we treat the person we will probably never see again shows us who we truly are. The key is to treat each and every individual we come across with kindness and respect rather than reserving this treatment for a special few. Who knows? Perhaps that moment of kindness to your janitor, server, or the person waiting in line next to you for a latte could turn their life around.

If we are patient and stay alert, we are afforded the opportunity to meet special people. Meeting Adrienne Bankert in February 2005 was one of my life's golden moments. Standing before me was a young, bright, special gift waiting to be revealed to the world. I was fortunate that day to be able to see into the future, able to see right where she is living today. She has turned into the powerful woman that I envisioned the day I met her.

Over the years I have had the privilege, in different cities, to see people come up to greet her with fondness in their hearts and a twinkle in their eyes. They speak to her like they were best friends. The warmness she lives while on air has always communicated her love and kindness to those watching. Most, if not all, of the stories you are about to read were never broadcast. One of my favorites is when her kindness was expressed as she was walking through New York City, stopping to speak to a young mother pushing a stroller with a baby, who, by Adrienne's keen observation, was having a rough morning. She made time to invest in this woman's life, encouraging her and telling her that she would overcome the challenges she was facing. As a result of this perchance meeting, that relationship continues to this day.

With an extremely hectic schedule, including coast-to-coast and international travel as part of her job, Adrienne makes time for others—every day and in any way, expressing kindness to both the fortunate and the less fortunate. Whether it is while working in the studio, riding on a plane, or walking in a park, she is ready at a moment's notice. I happen to know that a big part of why she is so intentional is because she is extremely grateful for the times people have been there for her. I have called Adrienne when *she* needed someone to encourage *her*. This life that she chose is not always easy, and people can be unkind. I am glad to have reminded her on those occasions that we're not going to join in with anyone having a bad day. I am so glad she listened and that she is now sharing these skills with others.

Adrienne is ever conscious that in our busy, overtaxed, and go-go-go world, people need to know that they count—that they are important and they do matter. You are about to start a journey; this book is a treasure map and a how-to guide into a lifestyle of kindness. You will see the benefits of kindness in a new light. Adrienne will tell you that as a child she wanted to be a superhero. Today she is, and you can be too. Through these pages, become a superhero of kindness, and a champion of considering others.

Let her life inspire you. Let your life inspire others.

—Bill Krause, Business Coach

CHAPTER 1

THE ASK: KINDNESS 2.0

There is a force that energizes us all with passionate purpose. This superpower leads to relationships without regret and draws out 100 percent of a person's irreplaceable identity.

There is an unbeatable superpower inside every one of us that is far greater than talent or tenacity. It supersedes strength and intelligence. It crushes selfishness, negativity, and doubt.

It will bring you to 100 percent authenticity, develop unfailing integrity, and help you build trust with anyone. It's something that every individual, and every corporation, needs more of today. Our world, companies, and communities are asking for something more of us than simply getting the job done. The ask right now is for people who know how to be kind under pressure. This is about more than merely "getting along" with people. Your hidden superpower—*kindness*—reveals the highest and best version of you.

Kindness Stops the Madness

Kindness is the answer because our world is so busy and intense. Inevitably, that can lead to short tempers, burnout, increasing anger, and defensive debates. Witnessing kindness brings renewed hope in humanity in the face of jadedness. Kindness keeps us sane when the demands of juggling work and relationships put us on edge and fill us with the urge to lash out.

We can cause irreparable damage when we are unkind, which can lead to becoming numb or unsympathetic—something none of us can afford. We all have the ability to "stop the madness" by being purposefully kind.

Kindness added to any endeavor is a magnet for positivity and a cure for the inevitable side effects of stress. Kindness is an anchor to the soul and the universal language of hope for the billions on the planet searching for meaning. Kindness is inclusive. Kindness displays unity. Kindness is beneficial for all and is mandatory for those who are seeking true success, no matter the goal. Kindness is the gateway to new relationships and opportunities. Kindness is what the world needs now more than ever.

Kindness Positions Us

A pivotal point in my career came while in pursuit of a job that would lead me to my goal of becoming a national news correspondent. While I did not have an agent at that time, I did have a mentor and coach. I also had a longtime connection with the president of a media placement and talent coaching firm who referred me to Cheryl Fair, the general manager of the Los Angeles ABC station. She was looking to hire a new reporter. For the majority of my career, I had been in the studio as a news anchor. I could read a teleprompter with ease and handle breaking news. Now, I knew I needed to demonstrate that I was able to report in the field as well, which meant getting in a news van with a photographer and being ready at a moment's notice for a mudslide, or an apartment fire, or any number of stories where you had to be quick on your feet and still as composed as your colleagues back in the air-conditioned studio.

It is a highly competitive industry and, for a lot of people in the news business, their strength is either reporting or anchoring. Few are exceptional at doing both. (*It is for this reason that another news executive would later tell me he would have never taken the kind of chance on me that Cheryl did.*) Lucky for me, when Cheryl called to tell me she was hiring me, even though I didn't appear to have enough in-the-field experience, she said, "Adrienne, I can teach you what you don't know. I can teach you how to be a great reporter or how to be a success at ABC. The one thing I cannot teach you is how to be kind. Our mutual friend told me she has known you your entire career and that she has never heard you say a bad word about anyone. That is what we need more of in this business."

Less than four months later, Cheryl introduced me to the executives who would end up putting me on national television.

This was more than just getting me a job; this helped me find my sweet spot. Massive doors that other people try to kick down can open easily for us if we pursue kindness. But it is much more than being nice. Because people assume they already know what it takes to be kind, it is rarely tapped into in an authentic way. In order to make it your superpower, you must know more about what being kind really means. Consider this Kindness 2.0. Just like the latest operating system for our cell phones, it is high time for an up-to-date understanding of the scope of kindness.

Updating the Definition of Kindness

Kindness has been relegated to a form of politeness when it is, in fact, the key to connection. Like all innovation, kindness needs to be studied and practiced in a deeper way or it will remain unintentionally hidden in plain sight. Word meanings have changed over the years, so choosing a specific definition is important. Throughout this book I will be using the dictionary that made Noah Webster famous, the 1828 Webster's dictionary. Webster defined kind as:

> **KIND**, *adjective*
> 1. Disposed to do good to others, and to make them happy by granting their requests, supplying their wants or assisting them in distress[1]

Focus on the phrases in this definition. Select what makes you excited. Perhaps it is "making others happy" or "granting their requests." There is a big difference between helping someone and making them happy! When you are kind, you provide relief, even for a moment. It is a breath of fresh air. When you're refreshed, you enjoy life more, which leads to more clarity. This helps you make better decisions, creating synergy, innovation, and fun. Kindness is the thing that will set you apart while improving the world all at the same time. Kindness is your Home button. There are massive benefits to being kind that go beyond the notion that what goes around comes around. When activated, kindness provides a specially tailored path to your unique plan for success, relationships, and fulfillment. You are going to think differently about how to assist people in their endeavors, which leads you to take unexpected steps to your own happiness and success that put you in the right place, at the right time. It opens you up to a whole new adventure!

I have heard so many times, "Well, what if I am kind and they just take advantage of me? I have to protect myself." It's important to also grasp what kindness is not. Kindness does not mean being overlooked and just letting it go. Kindness does not mean you will never speak up. It's unkind not to make a difference; it's unkind not to be who you were meant to be. It is unkind not to stand up for what you believe in.

You'll see from examples in these pages how kindness is a lifestyle, and how people grow in their confidence in dealing with us, knowing they're guaranteed a consistently positive and generous outlook. Even the grouchiest people will want to be around us more and enjoy it! In spite of difficulties and challenging personalities, you'll be inspired to see the reward of making people's days better. By honing the skill of being kind, it will eventually become second nature when you are faced with obstacles in life. We can choose to participate in divisiveness, or we can choose to be kind. Kindness has been my daily coach and trained me to determine who I will be and how I will act, regardless of other people involved or the situation.

There are times in life when I have needed a "confidence compass"—when I've wondered where I was going next or when I've wanted to quit because pursuing a dream seemed too overwhelming. Hard work is only one part of accomplishment; kindness has the ability to take us beyond our natural talents and fast forward us light years beyond experience.

Kindness Is a Win-Win

It is time to advance what being kind does for your identity. You'll learn how kindness is the key for you to "just be yourself." Being ourselves means being *whole*. Through kindness, we will see that we are each "the one and only," which eliminates comparison or competition. Kindness answers the question, what makes us so special? without edging anyone else out of the picture. When you know that you are worthy, valuable, and important for the betterment of others around you, you will *act* better. The more people you impact, the more people look to you for support and kindness. In turn, as you exhibit your truest self—your kind self—you transform into a more engaged, present, and happy you. You being real helps others to discover and maximize who they are.

When you are real, you can combat cutthroat and cancel cultures by creating a positive environment. That is how we change the world: we pursue and embrace realness. When you're kind, you become unapologetically extraordinary in many ways. In these pages, you will see what it takes to be exceptional and down-to-earth at the same time. I highlight some of the powerful people I have met who have risen above negativity and refuse to deny the world the unique gifts they bring to the table. My hope is that everyone who reads this will, perhaps for the first time, feel at home in their own skin. You're going to become comfortable in your greatness.

Being kind not only showcases but produces a healthy

self-esteem. The more influence you have, the more you need kindness and generosity to be your safeguard against becoming demanding, arrogant, or harsh. Kindness keeps us grounded and relatable to all people as we soar to the heights we are reaching for professionally and personally.

Kindness produces the timeless power of a reputation, where people in your circle associate your name with being remarkable. A strong reputation adds indispensable value, which leads to a kindness legacy. My mission for you is to arrive at a place where you live convinced your actions affect those around you and those who will end up following in your footsteps. To know that you are that impactful is a form of kindness. We live in a time where any one of us could appear online, and anything we say or do could go viral and be seen by thousands or even millions of people. Whether you're content to be behind the scenes or feel most comfortable on a stage, there is a huge benefit to making both kindness in general and the specific acts of kindness other people do famous and widely known.

Just as we commit to following the latest diet or regularly going to the gym, we should make it our aim to be kind. It is nourishing and leads to better health, greater growth, and improved quality of life. Kindness can be developed like a muscle. Kindness has no age limits, restrictions, or adverse side effects. It is collateral that leads to some of the most generous charitable gifts, the most lucrative business deals, and inexplicable opportunity.

Kindness Makes Moments Count

Kindness produces elevated conversation and gives meaning to human interaction that would otherwise be obligatory or taken for granted, turning brief moments into impactful impressions. I once attended a book signing and watched as the author greeted the guests and the children of those who attended the event. These kids had not read his book, but they were powerfully drawn to him. The author captivated the whole room with his graciousness, looking everyone in the eye as if they were the most important person in the world. It reminded me of something I read in a book about Mother Teresa, that when people met her, she made them feel like they were the only person in the room. Kindness shines a spotlight on others, without diminishing our own brightness.

How many times do you pass people in the hall at work and just say, "Hi" or "How are you?" and keep moving? A cordial hello is simply not enough to build relationships with colleagues. Instead, engaging in meaningful exchanges will make the workday far more interesting and productive, and can even carry you through difficult times.

Yet it only takes seconds to express that you care. Once, one of my extremely busy managers gave me his usual, "Hello, Adrienne," in the hall. After I had passed him, in the midst of another conversation he was having, he stopped to ask, "Adrienne, are you okay?"

I was shocked that someone had noticed even a tiny bit of the stress through my usual smile. In that moment, my home and my job were in a time of transition. I was certain things needed to change in my life, yet I didn't know how to make those changes happen. My manager's concern snapped me to attention. Although there was a lot of uncertainty, life was good; I just needed to let go of the anxiety. It was kind of him to be so perceptive, let alone ask me. Those words alerted me to change my attitude and replace being overwhelmed with optimism. It didn't take much, and it didn't look like much, but he was being sensitive, and I needed a reminder to relax and know that everything was going to be okay.

It's easy to minimize these seemingly small moments, but you're going to see how all these times where someone reaches out to you, and vice versa, start to add up. It is very easy to start thinking negatively when you are surrounded by negativity, which has become all too common today. Yet I know that you will get out of reading this book the same thing I saw while writing it: kindness makes you more aware of kindness.

When I began to examine kindness, kind videos started trending on my social media accounts, kindness campaigns were suddenly everywhere, and people were doing kind things for me and others around me all the time. While on a walk in New York City one morning, this question came into my mind, *What if no one had ever been kind to you?* I imagined where and who I would be if I had not seen kindness extended to me. My gratitude swelled for all of the times someone was a difference maker. If I had experienced zero kindness, I definitely wouldn't be who I am today or be doing what I am doing now. Seeing the world from this perspective brings far more joy as we start looking for and, most importantly, start initiating this superpower.

Kindness Is a Force

Kindness shown to us can compel or confirm that we are headed in the right direction. One day when I was in the office, I saw one of my producers and thanked her for sending me encouraging emails. Kelly had sent me a few notes while I had been out of the country on a multiweek assignment in Asia. On a trip like this, far away from home and in a whole different time zone, it is easy to slip into a feeling of isolation. We were in front of a camera for hours at a time, surrounded by media outlets from all around the world, fenced into (rather, crammed into) a small space beside street vendors and roadside restaurants. It averaged 90 degrees with 90 percent humidity, unless it was raining. On top of that, there was a fourteen-hour time difference from New York, so we were up late and back at it again early every day.

"You know," Kelly replied, "people are doing a great job, and we have meetings where those who did the work are not getting any of that positive feedback because they are working so hard, or in another time zone, or sleeping after being up all day. I know it's hard to be away from home, especially for a long time on the road, and I just want to pass those gleaming reports back to the people who did the work."

The fact that she sensed how I was feeling and took the time to send an email spoke volumes to me. I saved them all; they meant so much to me.

One read:

> You are crushing it. So captivating. It is so clear that you are so much more than a journalist. I can feel your compassion through your reporting. THANK YOU SO SO MUCH FOR EVERYTHING today!

This note not only made me feel appreciated, it was an affirmation of a goal I had made for my career from the beginning, which was to deliver compassionate and compelling journalism. Her note wasn't just nice, it was powerfully kind.

Being kind is a game changer on the job, resulting in employees who are invested because they know their value. You'll succeed in building a career with compassion, have a team that no longer finds "soft skills" hard, and enjoy a life of generosity and impact. It will also lead to radical connection. Genuine kindness changes a normal atmosphere into rarified air where we are engaged and aware of the strengths of others in the room.

I recall the first time I met *Good Morning America* anchor Robin Roberts. I will never forget how she gave me a hug, and then stood back, looked at me with those captivating eyes, and said, "You fill the room."

It was a powerful statement. I smiled inside, knowing how far I had to come to get inside these rooms with powerhouse people. I reflected on how it took more than a village, it took an army for me to arrive! All the hopes of every teacher, coach, mentor, family, and friend who believed and invested in me is with me on this journey. Wherever we go, we carry with us the people whose love and kindness brought us to where we are today. Kindness envelops the generosity and lessons of every person who has touched your life and gives you much more than you could have ever accomplished alone.

It's kindness that will give you a powerful purpose. You won't just make an entrance or impression; you will fill the room.

Kindness is more than the golden rule; it is a *superpower.* And amazingly, it is within reach for every one of us.

It is time to change our perspective.

CHAPTER 2

THE KIND: POWER TO BE YOU

KIND, *noun*
Nature; natural propensity or determination[2]

Most of us have experienced a time of losing ourselves, forgetting who we are, or not knowing who we are in the first place. For some it might have been the years between childhood and young adulthood, or as we approached thirty, or some sort of midlife, midcareer crossroads. You can remain anchored to your authentic identity by being kind. Kindness is the surefire way to replenish your purpose by reuniting to the highest and best version of you.

Let's first answer what is a tough question for most people: WHO ARE YOU?

It's not about what you're good at, where you've worked, or

what your friends say about you. I want to know if *you* know who you really are. I ask this because, like many of us, I have heard the words *Just be yourself* my whole life. It was the answer whenever I asked someone more experienced than me for advice. It was the answer when I wanted to know how to be really good at something:

"*Just be yourself.*"

In the beginning we have enough raw tenacity to go out and try whatever it is we are after, even if we have no idea who we are. Our youthful ambition is enough to get us in the door. That ambition can wane over the years when we don't reach the milestones we think we should by a certain age, or after having a certain amount of experience, according to our personal timetable. Let me give you some examples of things we tell ourselves we should be that end up falsely defining us:

- I should already be making six or seven figures.
- I should have been named a partner at thirty.
- If I am not married by thirty-five then ________________________(fill in the blank with half-hearted plan B).
- It's too late; I'm too old to start over.

When we don't hit certain milestones—and the further in life we go without achieving them—we may end up defining ourselves based on what we have not done yet. We become our own worst critic. As we go through life, every time we hear the words, *JUST BE YOURSELF,* it eventually becomes a barometer for just how much we don't know what that means! Many have no idea what makes them uniquely qualified to be special or accomplished, especially when it looks like they have not done enough. Fortunately, along the journey of discovery we learn more and more about what we want to do in relation to what *kind* of person we are or at least the *kind* of person we want to be. Here's the golden ticket: my first answer to, "Who are you?" is always, "I am kind."

When things seem blurry, or I feel my passion lessen, or when I do not feel as secure in who I am at the moment, or when I don't know what to do next, I remember I AM KIND. I may feel lost, yet I have not lost *myself.* This never fails to orient me.

Knowing I am kind, it becomes easy for all of my actions, goals, values, and thoughts to be aligned even when things seem really, really hard. *Kindness is not just what you do, it's who you are.*

I want you to see kindness as more than a task or description. I want you to see it as a state of being. Let's go back to the definition at the top of the chapter. *Kind* as a noun is defined by Webster as, "nature; natural propensity or determination."

You seeing kindness this way will help you understand your identity. Once kindness becomes your identity, it will increasingly rule your thoughts, actions, and deeds. No matter your background, ethnicity, age, or income level—if you are on the planet, you are eligible. By identifying with the nature of kindness, we have a "determination" and a "natural propensity" to heartfelt benevolence. This will produce a true and pure form of generosity.

KINDNESS IS A STATE OF BEING.

Kindness leads us to the next factor in the equation of identity, which is, "How are you different? What makes you so special?"

To discover your uniqueness, start with the intentional choice to be kind. Your individual kindness is like your fingerprint—something that cannot be duplicated in exactly the same way, leaving an indelible imprint on the people you cross paths with. Once we choose to make kindness our focus in life, we will be assured that no matter our age, stage in life, or history, our vision and destiny are clear and our value is limitless. Decide, no matter what you do, you are kind.

Diane von Furstenberg, one of the most prolific and successful designers in the world, says to start with the *being.* In her book *The Woman I Wanted to Be,* Furstenberg wrote, "I didn't know what I wanted to do, but I always knew the woman I wanted to be."[3]

If you don't know what to do with your life, here's your answer: start with making an intentional, purposeful decision to be kind—because this is the person you know you always wanted to be.

I began to fully understand the power of kindness when I asked myself who I wanted to help right now and became deliberate in finding that audience. I stopped looking at wasted time, and mistakes, and what I felt I had not done. Instead I looked to a picture or vision of the kind of person I had wanted to become for years. I also realized how stressed out I was becoming over all the questions I felt I could not find the answers to for myself.

An aha moment came when I saw that millions of other people had the same questions. If I could go on a quest to answer the questions for others, I would automatically have the answers for my life. I started with what I did know, sharing the wisdom I had gained from experience and from people much wiser than me with whoever would listen. Being kind enough to share what you already have that works by teaching it to others unlocks new wisdom. Start giving what you do have, be it time, expertise, or a talent and share it! You will grow by teaching as you also see how much you have to offer. This will bring you to a greater understanding of who you are individually and where you fit in the bigger picture. When you are more confident in who you are, you have more power to decide.

Know Who You Are

I was talking to one of my dearest friends, Jules, who'd left a high-paying, notable career to be a stay-at-home mom. "I think I need to go back to work. Once I get a firm professional footing again, I will have the confidence to think about what I really want to do. I just feel right now, I'm not fulfilled or inspired," she said.

I love my friend and know her well enough to decipher that she was looking for her identity in her career. She was looking for a job when what she needed was to find herself. Maybe you've been there. I have. She *wanted* to do something completely original, and that scared her, so she was going back to familiar options. By playing it safe, she was not *being* her real self.

As I shared with Jules, knowing who you are eliminates a lot of overthinking, fear, and confusion about life. As we brainstormed some ideas for her going back to work, including returning to her former job part-time, consulting, or teaching, I explained that she has something priceless that cannot be revoked: her power to decide. Before she was a wife and mother, she knew *exactly* what she wanted to do. It was a career goal of hers to be a meteorologist and she quickly attained the dream. When it came to this, she told me, "I was not going to take no for an answer." One of my favorite stories about her knowing what she wanted was when she and I were working together, just before she got married. I asked her what she was doing for Valentine's Day.

"You know," she said, "I am going to make myself a nice dinner, have some wine; I have a feeling this is my last Valentine's Day single."

Within months she met her soon-to-be-husband and was engaged by the end of the year! Jules even made this statement about how certain she was that he was the one: "I just knew. The sky is blue, the grass is green, and I'm marrying Mark."

I reminded her of her own words. The fact is, the sky is blue and the grass is green. I told her that the fact is, she needed to do a new thing! One thing that makes people attractive is a healthy self-esteem, which comes from a clear knowing of our vision and our mission in life. When you know where you are going, a peace comes over you that replaces worry, anxiety, and fear. But now my sweet friend Jules—who knew exactly what she wanted at the start of her career and in love and marriage—was hesitating over what she wanted in life because she hadn't made that same focused decision to choose to be true to the real dream inside of her and the kind of person she was *after* kids and marriage. Finding her way back to the confidence of making a bold decision was not easy. The problem is when we are confused, or don't know what is next, we can't even be honest with ourselves enough to know what we want.

Jules finally made the firm decision to take some time away from her career. She found a *different* kind of fulfillment staying at home, while remaining eager to find her niche. It wasn't long before new opportunities popped up as she stayed true to her heart and connected with the community. Today she is as busy as ever, with freelance work that allows her to have more time with her family.

Over the course of this journey, when Jules would talk to me about her doubts and fears, I would remind her that she had something priceless: a great reputation. When you are being who you are called to be, it's going to demonstrate itself in a way that others notice. People will see that intrinsic value. I asked her to make a list of all the people who know her and would help her. Why? Because they just love *her*. She has become known for being a sweet, funny, smart, awesome woman, and a lot of that cannot be quantified. There are other sweet, funny, smart, awesome people, there just isn't another Jules, and they love Jules. People in the community wanted to work with her because of that kind name she had made for herself, by *being herself.* Kindness brings out the best in us, the undeniably real us. The true you shines through. What others notice, from your next-door neighbor to your next employer, is not just that you are capable, but how you treat people.

The Power of Decision

What Jules's story taught me is that whenever I had my own doubts and fears, and felt I wasn't going anywhere, it was because I had not made my decision crystal clear. In those times, I hadn't worked on specific, tangible, measurable goals. I had been less intentional about how I wanted to live or give my life to others. I was not being kind to who I was as a child, the little girl who imagined great, big dreams. I was being un*kind* and disloyal to myself. To get back on track, I needed to put who I wanted to be kind to back in focus.

START WITH WHAT *KIND* OF PERSON YOU WANT TO *BE*.

The kindest people I have met have had ups and downs. If you took everything they possessed away from them (family, health, house, money), they would still be kind. Start with what *kind* of person you want to *be*. Do you want to be the kind of person who cheers others on when they are doing well? Focus on that. Do you want to be the kind of person who pays off people's mortgages and utility bills as a surprise gift, just because? Focus on that. Do you want to find a solution for homelessness or a cure for cancer? Take time to dream about that. Do you want to be the coworker who brings in freshly baked cookies every month to the staff because it lifts morale? Do something with that.

Wait—do you think of warm impulses like this but don't do them? Or would you tell me you aren't sure where to start because you don't have the resources? Deciding to be kind may require you to add to your vision board—which may be full of images of your dream vacation, car, or wedding—a detailed picture of intentional kindness. Add a few carefully selected images that illustrate to you what being kind, generous, and thoughtful to the people in your life looks like. The world is ready for your life-changing benevolence. You might have to do what I did and put the word *kind* up on your bulletin board. You might have to take some time and research the kinds of things you want to do regularly, and then put them on your checklist. I created different categories and noted them below. This will maximize your time and produce energy that you're investing that time wisely:

- Go to the gym Monday, Wednesday, and Friday (kind to my body)
- Buy coffee every third Monday for a stranger in line (kindness to strangers)
- Bring a treat to work once a month for coworkers (kind to the team)
- Put $50 a week into a fund for charitable giving to a cause you care about (kind to the world)
- Take time, without interruption, to work on your goals (kind to my purpose and future)
- Call up business associates "just because," or send them a gift or flowers when you know they are going through a stressful week (kindness to colleagues)

- Schedule a nail salon appointment or staycation at a hotel for a slumber party with your friends who you see less often because you all are on that grind (kindness to your inner circle)

These are simple examples to jump-start your ideas around kindness as a lifestyle. Start here and expect it to become more organic as you see opportunities around you. It starts with little things. Then it becomes a part of you and keeps you kindness centered.

Be Loyal to Your Conscience and Trust Your Gut

For true authenticity, it is important not to betray your conscience. When you add kindness to the mix, you will be able to make a decision from the heart and more readily trust your instincts. You won't just go for what looks good; you will know what is *right*.

EMBRACE KINDNESS; IT WILL HELP YOU PAY ATTENTION TO YOUR CONSCIENCE FOR OTHERS' BENEFIT.

Every one of us has a values system, and there are many times in our life where there is a crossroads. If we are not careful, we will be in denial of aspects of our lives that need to change, mainly because we are not used to living by our conscience. The sound of our own desires, spoken by our voice, can become muted because we start to make choices based on the bills we need to pay, what we feel we can control, or what we think is demanded of us. For example, you might know someone who enjoys their career but dreads weekends, when they punish themselves by hanging out with people they have outgrown and don't even like. When you are lonely, you may overcompensate by working too much, eating too much, or use other vices in attempts to fill the void. You may have friends who have a huge salary and a beautiful home but are unhappy, yet they refuse to change because they are too comfortable.

How do you avoid compromising your own standards? Embrace kindness; it will help you pay attention to your conscience for others' benefit. You will become an expert in trusting your gut. Instead of being motivated by loneliness, obligation, or any number of preferences, kindness removes judgement. By developing an inclination to do what is right without overanalyzing all the facts and stats about the person you are helping, you will become more practiced in sensing intuitively what is right for your own life and develop the courage to make changes with the proper motivation. You'll know what is right, right now.

You Make the Day Better

I make it a practice to send thank-you cards, emails, or DMs—I also know the everlasting power of a handwritten note—reminding people of how grateful I am they were kind to others. In the spirit of gratitude, one recipient responded with a note that said, "You make the day better." I think that's about the best thing you can hear someone say about you. When someone comes alongside us to help us make it through the day, there is hope. People beside us, in the next cubicle or next door to us, give us a sign that it is a good day, and everything is going to be all right . . . like one of our longtime stage directors at *Good Morning America*, Eddie. Eddie has tattoos down both arms. One forearm reads *forgiven* and the other reads *blessed*, so that when he points to your camera, you are faced with those words. He is always laughing and smiling. Even when he is tired, he remains upbeat. One day he seemed a little deflated. He still made the time to ask me, "How are you today?"

"AMAZING!" I said enthusiastically, hoping to boost his spirits.

His priceless response was a song, as he belted out, "Ah-mazing Adrienne, how sweet the sound," to the tune of the song "Amazing Grace."

He made me feel like a million bucks. I will never look at that song the same way again. Eddie, you make the day better! Here's to you and all the other superstars who help others shine brightly, exhibiting encouragement every day by being the kind who are *kind*.

CHAPTER 3

SOMEONE IS ALWAYS WATCHING

> Someone is always watching . . . even when you can't see them.
>
> —Mom

Some memories from my childhood remain deeply embedded in my mind. I'll never forget changing my siblings' diapers or the thrill of learning how to make authentic Mexican food from our next-door neighbor. Another thing that has followed me into adult- hood is that every so often my mom would say, "Adrienne, someone is always watching." My mother was constantly reminding me to set a good example in front of my siblings. She couldn't be there all the time, and her intention was to help me develop a strong sense of right and wrong, and a conscience that would be sensitive to my behavior and choices. Those words became a mantra for me, and, to this day, I endeavor to act in private the way I would act in public. It is not always easy, but it has led to my being the same person on air and off, which is what I always wanted. (Thanks, Mom.)

What we go through in the formative years of childhood will either develop confidence or fear in us. One thing is for sure, children act differently when they know someone is watching them. While I am not a child psychologist, I have made some observations from time spent with others' children (first in my large family, then growing up as a babysitter for other families). I've seen how children act up or straighten up when they know someone has their eyes on them. Some are natural performers who will put on a show to be the center of attention. But most children straighten up when they know someone may not be pleased with whatever it is they have in mind. They might smile, act shy or guilty—but they immediately change their behavior upon being seen. Even if they do not know the one they are being watched by very well, they adjust when they perceive an authority figure. If someone makes eye-to-eye contact that signals, *I know what you are doing*, they can quickly change course. When I speak to parents, they tell me that knowing their kids are looking to them as role models changes their own behavior. Whether a parent or not, when we are mindful and aware, we tend to change our behavior for the better when we know someone is watching. It helps us to make different choices.

Not Everyone Will Truly See You

We all inherently want to know that someone truly sees us; that someone believes we are special and that we have their attention. The problem is that after years of hurt and disappointments, some of us don't believe anyone is paying attention. On one hand, we can lose focus of how we affect others. On the other hand, there is the problem with not doing anything about who we do notice. Too often we either don't recognize that someone needs our attention, or we feel we cannot do anything about the coworker who is depressed, lonely, or in need of a pep talk or a smile. When we are the one in need of that encouragement, it helps to know someone is aware of us enough to do something about it, and it can be a breakthrough or a real lifesaver. It's up to us to choose to pay attention to others.

Some of my greatest audiences consist of thirty to fifty people. You can't see all the men and women who are working behind the scenes to put *Good Morning America* on television. And I cannot see all of the crew who are listening to everything I say. That invisible crew is busily working, but they could look up and see my face when something happens, like they shorten my airtime or insist on changing a line in the script. I like to assume they see and hear everything! I often ask the director, "How are we on time?" My theory is it's my job to help the director stay on time, not the other way around. I am thinking of the people who I can and cannot see, and I am thinking of the whole half hour of the show and not just a couple of minutes in my segment. Here's the point: *Being kind by realizing someone is always watching will make you constantly aware of a bigger picture.*

BEING KIND BY REALIZING SOMEONE IS ALWAYS WATCHING WILL MAKE YOU CONSTANTLY AWARE OF A BIGGER PICTURE.

My mother's words that someone is always watching had such an impact on my ability to stay composed and kind under pressure. As a journalist just starting out, I saw that some people, after having worked for years in the sleep-deprived and intense working world, became harder, more jaded, and terribly cranky. My business coach has counseled me to be gentler, more patient, and more gracious every year. He has told me, "I want you to be calm, whether on a full night's rest or just one hour of sleep."

I admit it's one of the biggest challenges in my life to not let my circumstances dictate my response, but it's been worth it. Practicing this is a form of discipline just like lifting weights or intermittent fasting. I talked to a Navy SEAL once, and he said the way they train in the most difficult conditions prepares them with the response that will come automatically under the greatest pressure. Think of disciplining yourself in kindness as a form of personal training and developing muscle memory.

Training is different than trying too hard. When you are insecure, you're concerned you will make a mistake and worry about being caught saying or doing the wrong thing. Living with the consciousness that someone is watching all the time, when handled from the right perspective, causes a growth spurt of security. As a child I would often think I might get in trouble for something someone saw me doing—from the cars that would drive by to the people at the store. The problem was that with each passing year, I was increasingly concerned with what people thought and making sure I did everything right. It was much safer in my mind to be poised and polite if it meant I kept myself from making a mistake. You might be like I used to be and insist on not making a mistake. This doesn't work, it just makes for being too uptight, constantly in your head trying to please people, and being someone who never is free to be themselves.

Thankfully, I grew out of the method of publicly hiding behind a type of perfectionism by growing in my career. The pressures of *getting it right* in those precious moments of a live broadcast, and yet having to get over mistakes made that I could never recapture if they did air, helped me to stop trying to be perfect and focus more on being myself.

Television gave me a method of being fearless and authentic so that I could get a vision for being assured I would make right decisions and not be motivated by a fear of blowing it. In TV, the show must go on. Even if there are wild things happening behind the scenes, those on camera remain composed. You have a script, but you stay flexible for changes. Consider your career (or any area where you feel sure of yourself) to be a tool to bring you to the highest and best version of you in every area of life. The confidence you build in doing your job well can be translated to other areas. When you choose to believe you will make the right decisions, even while being watched, you build up your expectations for good results.

That is why training from coaches and mentors is so effective; it creates a safe cocoon of accountability within which to research and develop. Practice makes perfect, and you can talk through how to handle certain situations and get feedback, translating that to more and more of your real-time experiences. By having a partner to witness your wins, you are better able to capitalize on your unique gifts and personality with kindness, compassion, and consideration for others. Being truly seen by people who could recognize my gifts helped reaffirm me when I had to stand on my own with everyone watching.

How to Act When You Notice the Unkind

When you are on this mission to be more watchful, you'll inadvertently notice when people are less than kind. From the customer service on a plane or the sternness of someone's voice, to blatant disrespect, we don't have to go out of our way to notice someone being rude. I've discovered it is not our job to fix that person or correct them. It only makes things worse.

One day I spoke with a woman who had a terrible situation happen after using a rideshare app. She had opted to use a carpool feature. The other passenger in the vehicle was extremely rude to the driver and this woman was trying to stick up for him, which led to an all-out fight. My advice to her was that when people's tempers are raging, it makes no sense to jump in the middle. Just because you are seeing things right, doesn't mean the other person will agree with you. Instead of trying to bring the error to the offender's attention, distance yourself from the person who is causing the conflict. Follow up with the person who is being treated unfairly. Tell them, "I apologize on that person's behalf," or say, "Please forgive them. It's not right how they treated you and I hope that you are OK. Don't let this ruin your day." This may not stop the perpetrator of callous behavior, but when you cover it with kindness, you have a chance at preserving someone's peace for their day. They will be encouraged to know someone noticed and cared enough to speak up.

Someone recently said something unkind to me on the job. I surprised myself with the calm I had; I was not defensive or even ready with a rebuttal. Believe me, at one time in my life I would have replied and told them exactly how I felt. As you practice kindness your temper is often eliminated. That trigger to anger first wanes, then disappears. I smiled, walked away, and realized I was glad I wasn't going to be insecure about their insecurity. I didn't gossip with coworkers about what they said; it would not bear repeating. Instead I held my tongue, knowing that the unkind person didn't know themselves or me at all.

Their ignorance of me doesn't stop or deter me from the power or promotion in my life. If I were to speak up, argue, or complain I would be fighting on their low level.

Correcting them for their fallacy wouldn't help. In fact, it could start a war. The good news is that their disrespect prepares you to know what you may experience when you work with them in the future. Know your players and know there is a power in silence. Be the more mature person and don't allow yourself to hold a grudge. Some are watching you to see how you'll respond to their jab.

Follow the Impulse to Help "Just Because"

I was sitting in my office one afternoon when one of our directors walked by and asked how I was doing. He always had a pleasant smile and something kind to say when he came by. He stepped into my office with a decidedly serious tone.

"I have to remind you of something you did six months ago," he said.

Six months ago? I couldn't guess what he was about to say.

"One of the women who works with us, her name is Betty, she was hobbling down the hall with a knee brace, doing everything to walk on her own, holding on to the wall to brace herself. As you now know, she was getting ready to go in for knee surgery and you stopped to encourage her. That really meant a lot to her and I heard about it. It really touched me."

I sat there a little shocked and grateful.

"Thank you for sharing that with me," I said.

"You know we are all sharks in this business and so rarely do we stop and say anything nice," he said.

I interrupted him.

I NEVER TAKE BEING JADED LIGHTLY; IT IS A SIGN OF LOST HOPE IN HUMANITY.

"Not you and me! We're the exception! And more people are like us. We are starting a movement!"

He smiled. There are plenty of nice, good-hearted individuals who want to do a great job. More often than not, I hear them express without even realizing it how negative, distrusting, or misunderstood they feel. In every industry, we are so crunched by deadlines and travel and getting the facts and statistics straight! Think of your own office, whether you are in advertising, construction, law, sales, or education. There is universally a majority of people who will say things like, "Wow, so you're not jaded like the rest of us? Give it time, you're still young."

I never take being jaded lightly; it is a sign of lost hope in humanity. No matter how much we try to make it all about the day-to-day tasks or getting the project done, our careers are an extension of the people we are behind closed doors. It's impossible to completely fake it at work every clocked-in hour so that you are perfectly politically correct, emotionally neutral, and supremely unaffected every time you go to the office. This is unrealistic, yet there is an unspoken rule that some people abide by in their minds to just get by. Simply smile and do the job. I am sure you, a coworker, or client has expressed emotions in ways that are less than constructive, combined with frustration and stress in short outbursts that are easy enough to forgive, though many who witness these moments don't forget and may act like they just didn't see it. I've seen where people have been subliminally taught that it is better not to say anything. You may have been surprised when someone stops in the middle of their busy day and makes time for genuine kindness. I am thankful I have seen many instances from the team I work with.

What difference could you make by checking in with a coworker who seems upset or jaded?

Jot down what you would say. For instance, "Hey, I noticed that you seem down. Anything you need to talk about?"

____

____

____

On the Run

It does not have to take long to boost someone or be the one who takes the time to do more than watch. Here are some stories of others taking notice.

One of our senior executive producers was in the middle of back-to-back special reports, the moments in the regularly scheduled programming where you hear that breaking news announcement. I was walking from another part of the building and saw him run out and I said hello.

"Hi! I'm missing the birthday party!" he said, as he walked as fast as he could. "I just heard all the laughter from the other side of the wall and realized it was time."

It was wonderful that this man, who was in charge of an entire team of people who would need to be ready to go on national TV, would stop his day and run just as quickly to the celebration with cupcakes as he would to the director's booth for an announcement from the White House.

One of the women on my digital team had seen me a few weekends in a row in the elevator. I was usually in a rush to get to the morning meeting. In the few short chats we had, I found out she was relatively new to the company, and she had a very pleasant way about her. Months later I was sitting in my office and had left the door open. I was slammed with moving, I hadn't finished my taxes, I was trying to do some writing, fundraise for a charity, and work on a speech while prepping for a story the next morning to air on *Good Morning America*. I was feeling stress to the point that I just wanted to disappear. In pops the lady from the elevator. I looked up and smiled. She had this very calm look on her face that I was comforted by, and I was curious if she was there to ask me to do something related to Facebook because she had never stopped by my office before. I thought maybe I missed an email from the team. I didn't think I could handle another to-do item on my list. I smiled, hoping not to let on that I was feeling extremely ill-equipped to handle the amount of work I had in front of me.

GENEROUS GESTURES SPREAD JUST LIKE GOSSIP.

"Hey there. I just wanted to let you know, your Instagram account, with the quotes and encouraging messages and all that—keep doing what you're doing. Sometimes I feel like I can't handle what I am facing that day. Then you post something and it's exactly what I need to hear. I just wanted to let you know."

I sat there, beaming. Her compliment gave me a second wind. I was surprised and touched. Some of the busiest people are the ones we need to get to stop and reflect. Don't think they are too busy to talk to—slip them a note on a Post-it and leave it on their computer monitor. If you can get a word in, just tell them they are amazing, or stop by their office with their favorite cookies or tea. Your thoughtful gesture will be something that refreshes them and helps their productivity, which contributes to the success of the entire team. You also will impact company culture as you express the importance of this among your colleagues.

Reputation

What we do at work makes such a big impact because people talk in the office! Generous gestures spread just like gossip. What other people say about us goes far beyond what we ever could say about ourselves. Without a word, people are watching and listening, and they are making judgments about who they believe we are. We can't control what others think, but like it or not we have something to do with our reputation. What we are really like is being broadcast all the time, by our actions and by what other people say about us when we aren't even around. We might as well give them something good to talk about! This isn't about trying to play the game or enter into office politics or win a popularity contest. Many people like to be oblivious to the fact that people think a certain way about them, or just do not care what others think, or believe they can't control what people say about them so it's a lost cause. But the truth is you have the power to craft a reputation. This isn't spin or propaganda. With the power of choice, you can take more empowered actions. When deciding to have a say over what kind of person you will be and what people say about you, think about what you want written in your obituary. At the end of your life, people are going to be saying things about you. What I want you to realize is that people are already saying the same things about you while you're on this earth; they just aren't necessarily saying it to your face!

Here are some examples of things you want to have spoken about you *before* they are read from your eulogy! Choose to make them a kind of mission statement over your life.

- She lived with her whole heart.
- He always encouraged others to be their best.
- She was an adventurer who found giving to others was her greatest thrill.
- He built up others with his words and helped tear down poverty with volunteering.
- She noticed others everywhere she went, creating ways to bring people together.

This is why being kind is more powerful than it might appear.

In the grand scheme of life, we all want to do something of purpose. What you become known for adds significance and affects your community, which in turn affects the world. Think about this in your own life, from childhood on. We appreciate and remember the kind doctors and nurses. We imagine our favorite athletes or actors to be kind. We see the difference between kind and unkind family members. Kindness spotlights and accentuates the talents someone already bears. The world is watching for the one next on the scene who can change the world, come up with a cure for cancer, or eradicate poverty, and it is a bonus if that hero is also kind. Inside each of us is a seed for greatness, yet we determine that it's especially great if that next genius or prodigy or talent is also kind.

KINDNESS SPOTLIGHTS AND ACCENTUATES THE TALENTS SOMEONE ALREADY BEARS.

Kind takes someone who is gifted from good to great, from better to the best. The amazing thing is that we all can attain great kindness, but we first must value ourselves.

Your Worth Will Rise When You Know They Are Watching

I've learned that we all make a difference. Another thing my mom would say as I was growing up was, "Adrienne, use your power for good and not for evil." She recognized that her little girl was a powerhouse! We all can be. I had to learn to harness that power, which meant knowing that when I fought with my brothers and sisters, it would affect the whole house. Similarly, if I was helping get the chores done while working well with all the kids, that too would impact the situation positively as they looked to me as the leader. It works the same way in business. Make a conscious decision to realize people look to you when you raise your hand to provide a suggestion at the meeting. People notice how you treat the employees. You will value your time at a new level and value the time you take to invest in others when you recognize that others are looking at you. To those watching, you are a difference maker and a world changer. When someone is watching you and wants to be like you, whether it is your child, a junior member of the team, or a young executive who wants to switch careers, they are looking to see if your way of doing business will produce the level of fulfillment they are seeking. I would love to tell you that people will always look up to you because you are wonderful, or they respect you. That might certainly be true. But many people are looking for a solution to their problems. We are all living proof that we cannot do this life alone. Be someone who doesn't hide the fact that they are here to make a difference.

Unplugging in Public vs. Watching in Real Life

We can sabotage our own best efforts and desire to live out who we are because too often we are watching other things that lead to distraction from our purpose. In an era where everyone can unplug in public, listening to their own soundtrack while flipping through emails and using social media as entertainment, we can become invisible. We can be so preoccupied we fail to acknowledge the person who walked right by us. We become practiced in distraction. What if there were something life or death happening near you? Are you situationally aware enough to know that all eyes may be on you to be a helper or a peacemaker?

With all the clamor of fast-paced lives filled with work, kids' sports, school events, and an endless barrage of social media and devices and screens, it would appear that no one is watching. We lose touch with ourselves and each other so that it's not even expected that we would ever be noticed. We end up sending mixed signals in a world that is hungering more and more for kindness and compassion. We put up billboards and public school campaigns advertising that every single young person is unique, important, and powerful. At the same time, we declare through TV and film and our own blatant actions that we have less and less involvement in the lives of those we love. It creates a hypocrisy in our society, as we say one thing and do the opposite.

It is at this time that we need to allow our actions to match our intentions; we can take notice and we should want to. We must decide to say an emphatic yes to noticing the child, the stranger, the elderly, and the in-between. Community requires communication. It is not about political correctness or minding our own business. It is about caring enough to notice and take appropriate action in that moment. It's easier and vitally more important today than ever.

Here are some ways to be someone who is always watching:

View meetings and errands as opportunities to give. I had a meeting with producer Mark Robertson. He has secured interviews with some of the most famous people in history and has helped create some of the most-watched moments in television. As I walked up, he raised a large iced coffee. "I got this for you." This man is in demand 24/7, yet he was not too busy to think of me before I arrived. Start to be more conscious of what others may appreciate as a pleasant surprise.

As a practical tip, keep hand lotion, mints, or for those living in colder climates, an extra pair of gloves in your laptop bag or purse for the sole purpose of being prepared for the people you are meeting with. Keeping cash on you for tips is not just good preparation for you, it is thoughtful for whomever you might interact with.

See your actions at work as an invitation to visit new neighbors. Create a sense of belonging everywhere you go. One week I had so much going on that I came in on my day off. One of my fellow correspondents came in to chat and I was honored. I encouraged him about finding a new nanny. As we brainstormed ideas another correspondent walked by. Because she saw two of us talking, she hung out. Then another! Three of them ended up cozied up together on my tiny office sofa. It almost felt like a hangout in my living room. Work can be fun and feel like family.

Another fond memory I have was the first year I worked Thanksgiving in New York, and I was invited to a holiday party at the office. It was organized by the hair and makeup team and the evening news floor director. The ladies had transformed one of our conference rooms into what looked like a spread at a house party. Hanging out almost made me feel like I was at home.

My favorite memory from the holidays involving coworkers, however, is when I worked as a news anchor in Dallas. My co-anchor and his wife invited me to spend the night and have the joy of family around me that Christmas. I had to cover the evening shows and they understood I would not arrive at their house until after midnight. It was a party! They had wrapped gifts for me, and I opened them with their kids around the tree. Then we talked, watched the snowfall, and ate a nice, big holiday meal. Their kindness was unforgettable.

Imagine that everything you say could be headline news. I'm not here to determine your moral compass. I am here to get you thinking. You would have different conversations around the office, with your friends, and with your hairstylist if you knew they were being broadcast across America. You would think more carefully about what you are saying about people and to them. It's served me well that I don't have to turn any part of me on or off to do my job in TV. What you see is what you get. I never have to censor myself because I have made the decision that I will be the person I really am, on or off camera. The real me.

Make this a daily mantra: *I commit every day to choose kindness.*

CHAPTER 4

KIND VS. NICE: BEYOND DEFAULT MODE

Kindness is often misunderstood. It's not weak and it is never people pleasing. Ultimately, it's one of the greatest acts of courage.

Our attention spans are so short, we have even learned to abbreviate kindness.

Picture in your mind how we appear when someone is trying to talk to us, and we are looking down, buried in our text messages. I've had friends gently drop hints that when I went to dinner with them, I was on my phone much of the time. I hadn't realized it and now I sincerely endeavor to put my phone away at meals. We sometimes are so distracted we cannot even hear what the person next to us is saying, though if we sense their lips moving, we may nod in their direction so they do not feel completely ignored. Understandably, we all need to handle our business, but walking around distracted is wasted time we will never get back. Sadly, making comfortable eye contact and engaging with people all too often feels forced because we have become so accustomed to our *divided* attention.

Nice can be a busy person's attempt to be kind.

We've all seen a colleague, passing us in the hall, likely with little to no eye contact. We greet them once they get within earshot with an upbeat hello. Their response is, "Good," signaling that they didn't hear what we said. They thought, perhaps, we asked how they were, but with the level of busy in their day they simply defaulted to a safe, one-word response.

Maybe you are that person. I have been too.

I have been too busy to say more than hi, so overwhelmed with work that I barely hear what the person next to me is saying. It is in these moments that I recognize that I need to maybe take a step back and see if I am paying attention to other people in my life. Slipping into default mode at work is usually a symptom that we are in default mode in other interactions. If we aren't careful, we fall into nice as a go-to, which makes us less situationally aware than is beneficial. Saying hello in the hall is better than not speaking at all. Ultimately, we want to demonstrate kindness that notices the other person's condition and does or says something to lift that person or engage them to confirm who they really are. I differentiate the two this way: nice is being polite to people; kind is connection with people. Both can be conveyed without words and within seconds. Kindness ultimately lasts.

NICE IS BEING POLITE TO PEOPLE; KIND IS CONNECTION WITH PEOPLE.

Kind and *nice* are used interchangeably in the first definition listed in Noah Webster's *American Dictionary of the English Language*. Other definitions hint at the root meaning of *nice*, describing exactness:

> **Nice**, *adjective*
> 1. polite, kind
> 2. pleasing, agreeable
> 3. socially acceptable: well-bred
> 4. possessing, marked by, or demanding great or excessive precision[4]

When you study the word *nice*, you can see that it is basically about exactness and execution. It reminds me of how many of us act when we have our first internship or first job. We want to do everything right. Behind our nice twentysomething smiles, we are fragile, worried, and determined to make a good impression. Most of us are not secure enough when we come into this new environment to be our true, confident selves. Unfortunately, too many people increase in position, experience, and connections without ever developing the confidence to display social skills that are rooted in true kindness.

One of the biggest hindrances to true kindness is that we think we are already kind, or kind enough. If this is the case, then we won't even bother changing our behavior. The first step we need in being able to grow is determining that kindness is like love—it can be nurtured and is vast. Second, we need to learn from those who are already kind. A mentor or coach can help you know what being kind truly means. There are layers and levels to kindness and tools for maximizing its effects in your life. But here's the deal: I want you to desire being kind instead of nice because you will not only grow personally, but also so you are ready to be properly coached or mentored. Because nice will not cut it.

A Coach Can Elevate Kindness

I cannot tell you how many times I am asked for advice as to how to attain a healthy mentoring relationship. This is a surprising benefit to graduating from nice to kind: You will be more teachable. In general, coaching can be direct and to the point with no time for tidy etiquette. Using playing for a city league versus the Olympic Games as an analogy, world champions require a different level of coaching. Sometimes straightforward advice can seem less than nice. The people I have mentored have told me this! I would find out sooner or later that someone I was investing in didn't appreciate the way I expressed the truth or the advice I was giving. Don't expect nice from a mentor or coach who loves you too much to leave you at the level you are. They won't ever let you throw a pity party; they'll push you to get back up on your own and then run a second mile. I realized kindness can bring hard-to-swallow truth, correction, and guidance during a trial by fire. Sometimes this is the only way we learn. It sounds backward but a kind mentor or coach will walk you right into the flames in order for you to learn the lesson. (I promise you they will give you a fire extinguisher and a flame-resistant jumpsuit first!)

Kindness is honest even when it stings. It would be unkind to smile in someone's face and not tell them, for example, when they have a huge piece of spinach in their teeth. Kindness will bring you to share what is important for someone's life and future, even if it means putting the relationship at risk. Thank goodness for people kind enough to tell us the truth about ourselves!

Kindness also means listening more, relaxing in your realness, and being patient with those who are on a different growth track and timeline than you are. For what it's worth, gentleness is a huge part of being kind that I have grown in myself.

Sometimes my passion, coupled with the seriousness of the situation a mentee was in, would elicit a strong response from me, though my intention always was to bring the person to their answer. I've learned that a friend will accept you exactly where you are. They will laugh, cry, and then take you out for drinks. A mentor's honesty will not come off in the way an associate or friend would communicate to us.

That is one of the major reasons why kindness might at times precipitate confrontation. I used to think that meant a fight. In modern dictionaries, confrontation often has a hostile or challenging undertone. However, the root meaning, which has lasted for centuries, is to meet face-to-face. As we've discussed, one of the reasons so many people do not know how to be their true selves is they won't confront their own reality. They do not trust themselves or other people enough to face their feelings or hang-ups, and they think we should all just be nice. Nice can be used as a defense mechanism. For those who are nonconfrontational, being nice is a means to avoid conflict. Nice will never bring you freedom. Without getting together with someone who will be kind enough to address the good, the bad, and the ugly with you, you are incapable of fulfilling your highest potential.

Keeping Up Appearances

There are some people I call "too nice." Here's what I mean. Being too nice can look a lot like kindness but with a motivation to impress people, perform, get attention, or please someone else. I don't think they do this with bad intentions. I think they do this to avoid any kind of conflict they think will arise as a result of being more set apart. Kindness shines a spotlight on your uniqueness, and nice people do not always want to stand out.

You might be a terrific giver of kindness and a terrible receiver. You're happy with people just being nice to you because:

- you feel bad receiving anything more since your life is already great, or
- while you believe in kindness to others, you feel you should work hard for everything you receive, or
- you feel people judging you for the life you lead and hate the way that feels, so you subconsciously sabotage success in one or more areas of your life.

Because we don't want people to think we are "too good," we start to become our own crisis PR team, because we know our lives look "too good to be true." We might be more average in certain parts of life just to balance everything out. People are looking for the real thing, and we are so concerned with what they think of us that we send a mixed signal. This is usually rooted in some unresolved fear or insecurity, and it limits your potential.

You might see some evidence that you are being too nice (and not kind) to yourself and others by, for example, becoming romantically involved with people below your desired standard. They are the kinds of relationships that are safe because, in the back of your mind, you know they are never going to work out; however, you stay with them because you do not want to hurt anyone. We are passed up for jobs because we care more about being liked by our peers than the challenge and privilege of being promoted! We fear that if we climb higher, we will step on toes or make enemies. This isn't considering other people in a kind or benevolent way; this is worrying about doing things perfectly or not making a mistake or losing friends. This is being too nice.

In wanting to be nice and gracious, we can almost be too

deferential, too modest, too careful—and sometimes we forget who we are. When we flow with words of truth, we panic inside. The voice in our head falters, then stammers, *Was that too much? Did I cross the line? That could be perceived or twisted wrong. I better not say so much next time.* In my quest to be kind, I have sometimes questioned my own power and authority. We sometimes dumb down our presence in a moment of levity to project that we are still the same-old-same-old, even though that child grew up a long time ago. If you've ever been called intimidating even by the most well-meaning people, you may play down your talent or professional prowess, and it causes you to diminish yourself in other key relationships in life.

Unapologetically Kind

I want to give you a heads-up, because being kind, in the way that I am describing, will bring a better life. So we want to make sure we don't start feeling bad for the good vibes being kind brings.

I was talking to one of my friend's children. She is ten and a very generous, sweet, and loving girl. Her dad has a great job and her parents and grandparents are big givers. She has a wonderful family life, a beautiful home, and she gets great grades in school. I started asking her about some struggles she had been having with friends. She revealed that she was feeling bad because her classmates didn't have as much as her. Sometimes they were jealous, and it hurt that she felt rejected by some of them. I could tell she wanted to make everything better. She would give things to her friends, mostly because it's in her heart but partially to compensate, to try and fix things. Underneath it all, she told me it felt weird receiving from people, even her family, because she already had so much.

One night, I took her and her siblings out to eat and she made a big deal about me spending my own money to pay for their meals. This little girl, with such a great life, was feeling bad about it when she could have been enjoying her cheeseburger. This notion that we have to apologize for having good things happen to us starts very young. It is time to realize that being kind means, yes, people will be kind in return! We can also be unapologetically gifted, talented, fortunate, endowed, and kind at the same time, without feeling guilt for having parents who work hard and earn good money. Guilt stops us from being authentic.

WE CAN ALSO BE UNAPOLOGETICALLY GIFTED, TALENTED, FORTUNATE, ENDOWED, AND KIND AT THE SAME TIME.

Let me tell you about another little girl, who also felt uncomfortable about the life she grew up in. Ruby knew she wanted to be someone special. She was loved by her teachers, got good grades, and dreamed of traveling the world and meeting kings and queens. Starting at around twelve years old, she would use the same imagination to make up stories of where her dad worked, though in reality she never saw her father employed and was too ashamed to tell anyone. Her family was on welfare her whole childhood, and she regularly experienced verbal and physical abuse. Because of the shame of being raised in poverty, Ruby felt unworthy of success. She even felt unworthy of people's kindness. She overcompensated in her own way, driven to earn love instead of knowing she was loved. She struggled with her temper and emotions for years, having been accustomed to fighting. As a young adult, she believed power came from being in control, so she constrained herself with rule keeping, restricting who she really was. She became accustomed to hiding parts of her life. It was the kindness of others that eventually brought Ruby to unapologetically *own her story*; they helped her see that growing up the way she did was nothing to be ashamed of, but instead proved her resilience and tenacity. She grew up to model the kindness she was shown, regardless of the unkind pieces of her past.

Never let anything or anyone make you feel disqualified from giving and receiving kindness.

An Unexpected Benefit

Kindness . . .

. . . is going to show you where you need to be kinder.
. . . is going to show you where you aren't kind, but you are just nice.
. . . is going to show you where you are afraid you're going to be mean.
. . . is going to show you where you don't trust yourself.
. . . is going to show you where you overcompensate.
. . . is going to show you what you want.

Being more knowledgeable about real money helps you identify a fake twenty-dollar bill. Being more knowledgeable about real diamonds helps you identify crystal or cubic zirconia. As you grow more and more familiar with what being kind really means, this quality will reveal to you where you are truly kind, when you are being nice, and when you have been overcompensating because you don't want to fall into any rude or inconsiderate habits.

What Do You Really Want?

Being kind is not passive. It is not a "que sera, sera, whatever will be, will be" attitude, as Doris Day famously sang in the 1956 film *The Man Who Knew Too Much*. Kindness is not fatalistic or nonchalant in any way. It is not as though kindness makes you invincible to being bothered, because things will bother us! We do not like where we are, how people are treating us, or what we look like, and we need to know how to harness the power to express that at different points in our lives. However, we are sometimes paralyzed by the busyness of life, past mistakes, and just plain old not knowing what we want so that we let other people make decisions for us that we would not ordinarily agree with.

For years in television I would try to communicate what I wanted my makeup and hair to look like, and I would say it in what I thought was a kind way. Or I would tell the hairdresser or makeup artist, "You're the expert; just know that I like light concealer and I don't like extra-long eyelashes." Somehow, I would never fully appreciate my look, and it was frustrating because I didn't know what to say differently to get them to understand. I finally realized that no matter what I said, I couldn't clearly communicate what I wanted because I didn't know what I wanted. I didn't know if the natural look I was going for in real life would work with the television lighting on set. I had grown to the point that I wanted to listen to the stylists, to get their insight and respect their expertise, but it was because I wanted to make sure that I did not repeat a mistake I had made during my first national show appearance on *The Talk*.

While still a local news anchor, I was asked by CBS to guest host on the show. The set hairdresser had styled my hair, and I did not like it on one side. I was trying to explain this and even asked for the curling iron to style it myself, but I couldn't get it right. Someone I respected greatly came in and could sense that the hairdresser was about to be fed up with me. They told me I looked great, and to leave the hair alone. After we finished filming, they said I should have let the stylist do my hair the way he wanted, that I was still a rookie, and that the pros knew what looked good.

Now here I was, a seasoned veteran in a position to tell people exactly what I wanted, but I couldn't communicate with confidence. In an attempt to correct my previous mistake of trying to do it myself, I was now going with the flow, but it was like I had taken my hands off the wheel and now no one was driving the car. I had noticed it in a couple other instances, where I was not fully taking ownership. I did not want to be a control freak; I didn't want to be overbearing or demanding. I caught this habit in the smallest things. When I would have an intern or social media assistant edit my videos, I would say what I wanted and, when they didn't listen the first time, I would acquiesce, agreeing with an unspoken uneasiness, even to the point of saying, "Whatever you think" rather than give direction. I thought that, somehow, I was being kind by not saying anything. (Believe me, there are times that the kindest thing you can do is just stay quiet!) This was, however, a realization that I had not been clear about what I wanted. My passivity was due in part to being weary of trying to talk with people who would not listen. I also wrongly associated my passion and attention to detail as a part of the old, unkind me.

At times in the past when I've tried to play nice, I told myself, *Don't say too much or do too much or BE too much.* Or, *It's better not to make waves or stand out more than you already stand out.* If we are truly being ourselves, then who are we to question what we are doing? We doubt ourselves because insecurity, fear, and the past are lying to us. Because we have made mistakes or hurt someone's feelings or said something the wrong way before, we think we will do it again. We must recognize that since we care so much about making another mistake, it is quite obvious that unkind behavior isn't who we really are, otherwise we wouldn't care!

Kindness transforms us into genuinely caring people who enjoy seeing others thrive and succeed. Nice doesn't do that. Nice is more concerned about saving face and being accepted. Kind people do not concern themselves with what clique they are in or who likes them, because their plates are full with the projects and people they want to help, embrace, and make a part of a group or family. Kindness doesn't have time to feel lonely. I want you to remember that even though you may struggle with your feelings or personality, as you grow in this, don't lose heart. You will witness an evolution as you combine your pure passion with incorruptible kindness. By continuing to do what is kind, you will always get closer and closer to the real you. *Do not stop the process.*

Author Kent M. Keith said, "If you do good, people will accuse you of selfish ulterior motives. Do good anyway."[5]

There are people who are going to be skeptical of your kindness and think that you are a phony. *Be kind anyway.*

There will be times when you want to defend yourself when people presume that you have some kind of underlying reason for being kind, or they think it is an act. *Be kind anyway.*

Part of the reason we need to practice kindness everywhere we go—with strangers, to those at the market or dry cleaner, to clients—is so we have the bandwidth to be kind to those closest to us. Your biggest detractors may very well be those you love the most. You know you've reached the epitome of kindness when you can be kind to your family and those you live with. The people who know your past will try and test you to see whether your kindness is an act. You may fall, lose your temper, or say something that you later regret. As I've grown in kindness, I've been much quicker to apologize when I am wrong, ask forgiveness, and do my part to mend fences. It is not my responsibility to make the other person feel better or convince them that I am truly remorseful. It takes courage to admit when you have been unkind—and then get back to declaring that kindness is your lifestyle, especially when someone who knows you might have other ideas. Your commitment to kindness, while being patient with yourself, will begin to remodel you so that you make fewer and fewer errors. You'll get to the point where you couldn't stay angry if you tried.

A Kindness Moment

Once you experience the benefits of kindness, you will not try to control people or be too hard on yourself. Deciding to be kind will eliminate the attempts to have to keep up with an image, which is truly exhausting if you just think about it. You will consistently be the same person on and off camera, in or out of the office, at home, or with people you've never met before. It is how we treat people that cements our true character. It is the people we may never see again, such as the gate agent at the airport, the housekeeper in our hotel, or those who work with us on a regular basis who give us a litmus test. They are a checkup ahead of crucial interactions that may more readily reveal if we are cranky or kind. If you find yourself being a little snappy with the taxi or Uber driver, then you might want to take some time and encourage yourself before going into that big meeting or walking in the front door to your family after a long work trip.

The goal is to be kind all the time. For a boost, here is what I do if I need to get back in the "kindness zone":

- **Deep breathing and a calming moment.** You might be a little less kind because you haven't been taking the time you need for yourself. Even if it's for two minutes, find a place where you can be quiet. Put the phone down and take at least three cleansing breaths.
- **Grab a hot beverage.** I go for a cup of herbal tea or water. I find drinking something hot slows me down and stops me from overthinking.
- **Go to the bathroom and splash cold water on your face.** Smile at yourself in the mirror and tell yourself out loud something affirming like, "I am winning big-time today!" You'll smile at the thought of it, even if you feel silly saying it in the moment.
- **Tell yourself you've already got it made.** One of my big life secrets is to say daily, "This is the best day ever! I am the happiest girl on the planet!" Imagine everything you need in life has already happened, everything is working out for you, and all your dreams are coming to pass. When faced with a challenge, I envision myself as if everything is already taken care of, which makes the deadlines due now, seem doable.
- **Call a friend and give them some encouragement.** A lot of times in the past when I was having a moment, I would call and vent to someone. Sometimes it worked to talk out my emotions, but there were times I felt worse. I discovered I always felt better when I took the time to make someone else feel like a million bucks instead of rehashing my miserable moment. This works because you are affirming your kindness muscle and giving your conscience proof that you are on track.

Lifestyle Tips for Being Kind

Do you know what you want? If you are stuck, think about who you want to help in this world and what kinds of things bring out the compassion in you. Knowing who you want to *help* is often easier to determine than what you want to *do*.

When it comes to communicating what you want with your family, a boss, or staff, remember that kindness gives direction and feedback. As I mentioned earlier, in the past I was great at giving feedback to people who worked with and for me, but sometimes not so good at giving direction. Feedback is reactive, and giving direction is proactive. It's more fun to get ahead of problems by being proactive. One of the kindest things you can do for those who work for you is to create a list of what you want, what your ideal is, and the way you want it done. For help in determining what you want, find photos or images on Pinterest or Instagram that you can save to give yourself time to dream. If you need extra help, have a friend interview you with topics like:

- "What celebrity's haircut would you most like to try out?"
- "What is your favorite furniture store and color palette?"
- "What meals would you eat every week?"

Make it a game of getting to know yourself.

Are you already kind? Self-evaluation is a mighty tool, and consistency in kindness leads to growth in that area. Discover ways to hold yourself accountable. Track how often you've called your business contact or friends, just because. Set aside a budget for taking friends for a quarterly or biannual night out, your treat, or get tickets to see their favorite artist. Plan ways to show appreciation to family members outside of recognized holidays and schedule it on the calendar at designated times. Plan some way to make the office fun beyond buying donuts.

One thing I did when I worked with my executive producer in Texas was to plan an annual bowling and arcade trip. You can do something as simple as putting different gift cards to coffee shops and restaurants in a fishbowl and have each coworker pick a prize. Step up your philanthropy to another level by using dream/goal setting time to discover who it is you want to help next in the larger community. Kids? Families? Cancer patients? The homeless?

Short on time? Schedule kindness like you would a doctor's visit or fitness regimen. Consider it necessary to your mental, relational, and social health, as well as your fitness goals. Set reminders in your phone to have meetings with those you care about at a deeper level and for accountability. Wish people a happy birthday, and plan for regular rewards for your office staff.

CHAPTER 5

FAMOUSLY KIND: COMPETING VS. BEING KNOWN

Everyone has an audience. Rather than putting on a show or turning on the charm, we can live our truth by being known . . . for kindness.

I wrote this chapter after searching for an answer for how we could all be incomparable. We know everyone is special; it just has not been the easiest concept to grasp or impart to someone. What I found is that the power to be your one-of-a-kind self is harnessed by making kindness famous.

There is a quote from television personality Sam Levenson, who rose to fame in the 1950s as a television host, that is often attributed to Audrey Hepburn. The actress would share passages of Levenson's book, In *One Era & Out the Other*, with her family: "For beautiful eyes, look for the good in others; for beautiful lips, speak only words of kindness; and for poise, walk with the knowledge that you are never alone." Famous for films such as *Breakfast at Tiffany's* and *My Fair Lady*, Hepburn was also a well-known advocate of children and refugees. Some of her most powerful personal reflections are about being kind. She's inspired a model we can all strive for. It's motivating, partly because Hepburn is one of the most celebrated people of all time. While there were and have been many great actresses, Hepburn exists in our memory as being in a class of her own.

Whether or not you desire fame, or only see it as synonymous with athletes, singers, and movie stars, in some way we all want to be known. We can be known by the people we care about and who care about us. We can be known for our great talent, ideas, or inventions. Traditionally, you become famous for *doing* something significant. What I want to help you realize at a higher level is that *you are already inherently significant*. It is from this vantage point that we can tap into our superpower. Know your value, and you'll *be known* for being the ultimate you.

Your Best Self Is Your Kind Self

Even though it is not listed as such in any thesaurus, when we use the word *best* I want you to see it as synonymous with wholeness and completeness. This is important to seeing best as a definition for incomparable and 100 percent authenticity. When you've given the world the gift of the best (or whole) version of you, you are inevitably going to attract people. You are on the planet, placed in your family, and working at your company to deliver something very special: YOU.

One thing I am often doing is singing! These lyrics remind me of the focus of this chapter:

Baby, this is what you came for
Lightning strikes every time she moves.
And everybody's watching her . . .
But she's looking at you.[6]

These song lyrics can get you to dance, but when I hear them it makes me think of how we dream of having the power to do the impossible. The second line here made me think of the phrase "capture lightning in a bottle." Here's Merriam-Webster's definition:

capture lighting in a bottle, *idiom*
to succeed in a way that is very lucky or unlikely[7]

It can feel like your breakthrough is a long shot. Kindness gives you assurance that you are going to make it. Having that hope keeps you on the cutting edge. Kindness is your immeasurable IT factor!

We want to be lightning in a bottle, not a flash in the pan.

Kindness is a gift similar to the gift of song, strength, or intellect, except not all of us can sing or have a high IQ. We are *all*, however, qualified to be beacons of kindness. It is one thing that never fades and that the world is constantly seeking. Recently I interviewed a show creator who was talking about all of the people he hired to be the stars of his new series. They were all extremely talented and good-looking, and before being brought on to the project, he spoke to all the crew who saw these young actors interacting with one another on set. He asked them about whether they were people the crew would want to spend the next six months with. He asked those auditioning about treating people well. This show boss told me the make-or-break quality in the business of entertainment is whether a performer is a thoughtful person who "hangs up their own costume, treats the hair and makeup teams well, and is a nice person."

When we realize the power of who we are, then wherever we are, we are a lot more fun to work and hang out with. Kindness makes you more generous and brings you more peace and satisfaction. People will wonder how you're able to stay cool, calm, and collected in places that can be anxiety-ridden. Haters cannot stop you from being kind; being who you are in spite of opposition will get you noticed. You'll end up wanting to share kindness with as many people as you can as an ambassador, leader, and game changer.

Standing Out

Some people are terrified by the thought of walking onto a big stage during an awards presentation for the humbling moment of accepting accolades. It's a lot easier to quietly accept a certificate at work or get your name on the wall of your company for something like having the highest monthly sales.

I want you to imagine yourself at work and your associates coming into the office with more happiness as a result of your positive attitude. Envision those who have a sick relative, for example, being steadied by your comforting words, and coworkers having a healthier self-esteem because they know you believe in them. They enjoy coming to work more and in turn are more productive. You may not get an award, but that is not why you are kind. You are kind because of who you are and the overall success of others. People will begin to look to you and stop you in the hallways more often and smile at you when they see you. You will be someone they might email when they are in a bind. This is the power of impact. But please, I do not want you to get nervous about more work being created by your kindness; you are going to work hard anyway! This inevitable human connection is what makes your job the most rewarding. We can help each other have peace of mind in the midst of pressure. Others will learn how to be kind and end up being a huge help to you in return because you have modeled that behavior. It is our responsibility to practice acts of kindness and perpetuate a powerful domino effect.

Lead or Compete

We all heard the horror stories of what happens when men and women lose their temper and say things they later regret during a conflict on the job. The marketplace can be mean. Hostility usually comes as a result of fierce competition and a culture that instills in us at a very young age to validate or overcompensate. When we recognize ourselves as leaders instead of contenders, we start to cure the wounds of aggravated infighting.

Leadership is an interesting quality. This crazy world can make it seem like you've got to be bossy to be a boss. The notion of having everyone watching you is a cue to your leadership, but so is the idea that you are looking at everyone else.

Real leaders are aware of what is going on in their teams and in their families, and what they can do to make systems and organizations better. True leaders are in a category of their own because they are more concerned with helping others than making themselves look good. All too often people strive to do the right thing in order to be recognized for their accomplishments. If we are comparing ourselves to others, we are getting distracted. We have an epidemic of insecurity in our world today. We don't know why certain people are chosen to work on certain projects or be promoted in different ways. It is something we have zero control over. If we take the energy we might have wasted trying to figure out why things happen and, instead, use it to work on ourselves and help others, we'll be too occupied with making the world better to ever worry about what the next person is doing. Looking at our life or work as a competition, breeds insecurity that focuses on winning at any cost. When we are kind, we realize we've already won.

AMATEURS COMPETE AGAINST OTHERS. PROFESSIONALS COMPETE AGAINST THEMSELVES. REALIZE THERE IS NOBODY ELSE IN YOUR CLASS. HOW CAN YOU COMPETE WHEN NO ONE ELSE EXISTS TO COMPETE WITH?
—Bill Krause, Business Coach

Years ago, I made a purposeful decision not to compete with anyone in my line of work, knowing there would always be someone newer, smarter, and more experienced. Because I was convinced that I belonged, I knew there would always be room for me. At one point in my career, I had a longtime employee tell me, *"You're the new flavor of the month, but just wait. In a short time, there will be someone new and you will be put on the back burner. It happens to everyone."*

I know they were attempting to be realistic with me, but I wasn't worried about being replaced or fighting for my position.

Practicing kindness had started me on a quest for how we could be timeless. I looked to articulate how being unique could lead to a one-of-a-kind success by just being ourselves. Just like every major corporation in America wants to create an original product that is more than a flash in the pan, people also desire long-lasting success. I found that kindness is so mighty, it creates a heightened capacity for originality. You don't have to worry about who the next flavor of the month is when you're the flavor of the century!

WE WANT TO BE LIGHTNING IN A BOTTLE, NOT A FLASH IN THE PAN.

Jumping into kindness with both feet answered the question of *how* to be extraordinary without reducing everyone to mere rivals. If we have a strong sense of heart and, as I mentioned earlier, we know who we are, we will enjoy our work and not just have a job. Making a decision to invest in ourselves, so that we know our value, gives us the joy to simply *be*. Kindness clarifies our passion and purpose.

No Contest

The downside to a contest is that there are a few winners and a lot of losers. Many see their careers like this. The reality check is that in the old marketplace model of competition, there were only a few worthy opponents. Today, there are far more companies, brands, and people in the business world to compete with. From technology to media, farming to cupcakes, some people "play nice" and others fight. I studied how the most successful people would carve out a niche to differentiate themselves. Still, it didn't fully eliminate the competition model.

I considered how much smaller the world is online—where it was likely someone who would be considered competition in the old way of looking at business could easily be a friend, a like, even an ally on social media platforms. There is the demand now to get ten thousand followers, then one hundred thousand, and then one million or more. If a number is the main goal, then identity rests in an algorithm instead of actuality. Turning our gaze from the numbers to the people behind the numbers sounds well-intentioned, but it can also be competitive, because then it is about being the best at helping people. I knew it was about shining the light on me and you with evidence that we each are truly in a class of our own. I sought for ways to be confident in who I uniquely was while making it a win-win for everyone else I wanted to impact (not alienate). I knew there was only one me, and if I was going to help others it would be by being fully convinced of that. I started journaling about this and here is what I jotted down:

KINDNESS IS SO MIGHTY IT CREATES A HEIGHTENED CAPACITY FOR ORIGINALITY.

> Being kind is our identity and our goal. When we are kind, we are so content being who we are, the real us, that we don't need to validate ourselves. We are grateful and fulfilled at 100 percent of who we are without doing anything to prove it.

That is when the lightbulb turned on. This may sound way too simple, but being kind *eliminates* competition. It is no longer about what someone else has that you do not. In fact, when you no longer look to your job, charity work, or achievements to define you, you become so wrapped up in the *business of kindness* that you don't concern yourself with the rat race or the climb. If we all look to make kindness the brand, we are marketing, and become famous for being kind (our truest selves) in our neighborhoods and our communities, then we turn the focus to others without any ulterior motives. You know that progress and promotion come as part of the total package of being the *true you*. The battle is in keeping your thoughts straight and staying focused on your growth and development, rather than being driven by fear, anxiety, and what others do or say.

I WANT KINDNESS TO HAVE MASS APPEAL.

In order to make kindness famous, you want to be kind to the person on the street who has nothing to eat and the CEO or mogul who looks like they have everything, as well as everyone in between. A company manufacturing cars, tortilla chips, or laptop computers wants everyone to buy their product. Similarly, kindness is something that I want to have mass appeal. I know that kindness can be displayed in every country, on every billboard, and through every industry. You look around and aren't living in a fantasy, you can see the cruel or thoughtless treatment of people. You will now see that kindness is a cure for that maltreatment. You realize your actions matter, which eliminates unworthiness and low self-esteem. You aren't defined by how much money is in your bank account, your clothes, or your jewelry. You know there is a priceless and enduring value to being kind. When you know that your very presence makes someone's day, you act differently. You don't just show up to perform. You are there to be the difference. You are concerned about others.

Act Like Every Action Matters

I frequently say we are all broadcasting something. Today, with cell phones, there is a chance that your conduct will be captured and shared. It's more important to act as though what you do may possibly be seen by a larger audience that you intended. Being on television has made me more aware because I see the playback, knowing there are millions of witnesses to our words. Nothing is hidden, as today's ultra-savvy audiences can usually spot a phony or the real deal from a mile away. What a news reporter may do for one to three minutes of airtime is an analogy for the broadcasting we all do twenty-four hours a day, 365 days a year in the way that we react and treat others. I aim to live as though I have a live microphone on all the time. I have seen the humiliating moments captured when a person who believed no one was listening was caught off guard. I am conscious that a stranger walking by can possibly hear my voice.

When you are being your real and highest self by being kind, you are fearless, living your life exactly as you intended in public and in private.

Your Invisible Audience Is Real

I want you to imagine the invisible audience you're consistently communicating to today. Can you see the viewer on the other side of the camera or advertising campaign? Can you see the person reading your op-ed piece? Can you see the teens, moms, and friends logging on to see what photo or caption you just posted on social media? They are watching. They can sometimes feel when you're having a bad day depending on how flippant you are in your post or caption. I post very deliberately. If it won't uplift or inspire, I won't post it. When we know our worth, when we know we could be the difference maker, it is easy to self-monitor what we do instead of just doing whatever we want or feel. If you need accountability in this area, have someone take a look at your posts before you share anything publicly. This is what someone with a lot of influence or fame would do. There are things that work universally that we should implement no matter what our status in life. Whoever you choose to run things by should be a person you give veto power to; if they don't think it's a good idea, decide you agree with them.

WHEN YOU ARE BEING YOUR REAL AND HIGHEST SELF BY BEING KIND, YOU ARE FEARLESS, LIVING YOUR LIFE EXACTLY AS YOU INTENDED IN PUBLIC AND IN PRIVATE.

Who will you give veto power to?

____

____

____

Recognize Your Platform

On a recent flight I was watching the Mister Rogers documentary, *Won't You Be My Neighbor?* I sat up when I heard Fred Rogers say, "Television has the chance of building a real community out of an entire country."[8]

The power of broadcasting is rapidly expanding, with the

potential to create community all over the world. Kindness considers community and begins with the people immediately around us. By broadcasting kindness to any group, we become the channel, the satellite, and the communication tower.

How you treat one authentic connection is how you'll treat the thousands or millions who inevitably become the audience. You want to start to engage with your audience before it hits one hundred thousand. Too often we wait until we hit a milestone that matters to us; but by doing that, we minimize what we currently have. We say to ourselves, *I know I should have more*, instead of realizing that in a pool of 347 people or 3,500 people, there is someone you can reach.

I recently interviewed a group of women who are changing their neighborhood. They started out with a private Facebook group and it grew to three hundred people. By using a social media platform, they allowed everyone, most especially the introverts, to connect. They now have a monthly clothing swap, share fresh produce from their gardens with one another, created a neighborhood watch, and share fresh-baked bread and cookies at parties in the local park. When I interviewed these women, they told me, "This saved my life," and "We all needed real friends." When I asked what the magic was, they said, "*We all needed it, but someone had to be willing to ask.*"

Now they have regular block parties with this group of families and enjoy authentic connections. They invest in each other. These women have become famous in their neighborhood; they have a reputation for sharing and providing a safe place.

In media, fans or viewers who reach out to you are often people who truly care about the story. There is a lot to do in this world and being busy is rampant. For someone to tune into your broadcast to watch is a pretty big deal. They could be doing a hundred other things. If you're in local news, they have coffee with you every morning. They cook dinner or order takeout while listening to you every night. If you're a writer, they look for your articles in online magazines or newspapers or follow you on social media.

I have a very special person in my life named Mrs. Cindy who just loves a particular radio station. Cindy loyally listens to her favorite on-air hosts. She knows when they are battling health issues and is familiar with their family life. She knows every trip and event this one radio host talks about because she tunes in every night. Her favorite host and I knew each other from the community and had done some events together. We became even better friends because of Cindy's appreciation. I would get a call from her as a reminder to wish her favorite host a happy birthday. Once someone I worked with at my first station was on the show as a guest, and I received a call from Mrs. Cindy at 11:30 at night to wish them congratulations on their retirement. I was already in bed, but it was touching to be a part of *her* program. She considered all of us in local media a part of her family. It was such an honor to be connected like that, and it endeared me more to Mrs. Cindy and to my hometown.

Plenty of people desire to have lives of distinction, to be famous, or have prestige. My hope is that this chapter has inspired you to be *famously kind*. I have seen through watching others that I could be famous for being talented, smart, or beautiful, but all too soon it is an uphill battle. Fame can be fleeting; popularity is replaceable. I have witnessed some very famous people treated with veneration, admired for their long track record; other times, people hardly seemed interested. They were looking for the new, next great thing. It can be depressing to think that if you do reach great heights of achievement that only few attain, that star power is short-lived. However, kindness is timeless and unfading. Being famously kind never goes out of style, always brings a smile, and shines a light on others' gifts.

Being famously kind might not put you on the big screen (you may not even want that), but I guarantee that whatever you do, being kind will outweigh any other gift you bring to the table. It will be your alibi when accusations of your character arise and outweighs any mistakes you've made as the gift of kindness makes room for you! No one is perfect, but as we are intentional and recognize how many people are watching us and how much of an impact we have on the group, audience, and community around us, we will build an indomitable brand of trust and a sterling reputation money cannot buy. Even if you run into tough times, kindness will return to you. Those you have been kind to will return the favor. Being famous for being kind is an impenetrable force field that sets you up for long-range success and fulfillment.

When you apply kindness, you will be known for being a problem solver and a peacemaker. You'll have a reputation for being prepared mentally and emotionally for the most difficult situations. You will deliver a kindness breakthrough.

CHAPTER 6

KIND CONNECTIONS: BUILDING TRUST IN SECONDS

You can't fake it and you can't deny it. Being kind is something the most celebrated and influential people in the world quickly identify. It's one way they separate the real from the phony.

The best part of my job in television is connecting with people during interviews. It has taught me how to connect with anyone. I have learned to create an atmosphere of trust in a room within seconds of being introduced to people I have never met. You learn how to be yourself and develop an ability to be sensitive to others.

Every time I enter a room, it is about getting a read on what people are going through and whether it is best to be high energy or more subdued. You can sense the stress level if a publicist is nervous, a producer is bringing calm or chaos, or if a guest is tired. You learn how to decipher who the biggest influencer is in a group—the person whose trust it is most important to gain. You learn how to defuse tension, speak in different communication styles, and do thorough research about your guests. You learn to relax, because if you do it right, interviewing is not about you at all—it is about others and making them feel welcome or at ease.

Having these brief conversations led me to revelations on how kindness allows for anyone to feel free to be themselves, and how being kind has shaped the lives and careers of some of the biggest stars on the planet. You can use these stories as an analogy in your own business meetings, interpersonal communication, and client relations, no matter what position you hold.

A Star Is Born

One of my favorite interviews of all time was with the cast of *A Star Is Born*, starring Lady Gaga, Bradley Cooper, Sam Elliott, and a young man from the Bronx named Anthony Ramos, who made his big debut in the original Broadway production of *Hamilton*.

Anthony was the first person in the room, and my producer was enjoying a conversation with him prior to the rest of the cast joining us. I had so many things floating in my head in preparation, as I never use notes during my interviews. Instead, I memorize all the facts and backstory and then listen for the follow-up. My producer introduced us while I was doing my last run-through of memorization and said, "Oh, Anthony, you got into acting as a kid because of a high school drama teacher, right?"

Anthony proceeded to tell the whole story: how he didn't have the money for an application to an arts school and this teacher not only called him to have him come fill it out with her, but she also gave him fifty dollars to pay for it. He talked about how his older brother and a cousin were now pursuing acting because of how well they saw him doing.

Moments later, Lady Gaga and Bradley Cooper walked in. Bradley, as Lady Gaga affectionately called him, was very protective of his cast, and you could tell he wanted to preserve what they had built together that went beyond chemistry. I communicated respect for that in various ways. One thing I made sure to do was ask how to refer to Lady Gaga. She was the first to be seated and I had a moment with her one-on-one, before anyone else. I wanted to make sure she knew I honored this moment. It was no secret that the film was emotionally charged, and it was her first major motion picture. As the rest of the cast was seated, someone called her Stephanie, her legal name. I gently asked her whether that was going to be her name after her debut as a leading lady and in this interview. She smiled, and said, "You can call me Gaga; my friends call me Gaga," as she turned to Bradley for support.

"Call her Lady Gaga," he said.

It was not about being technical; asking permission was a sign of respect and set the tone that I wanted to be *invited in* to hear about this special bond they had achieved. Too often in work relationships we try to force our way in, using humor or charm. In less than three minutes, we established that this was going to be a mutual exchange. After kicking off questions with the leading actors, I asked Anthony what it felt like to work with such megastars and to be in this class of actors. He said he was "floating on clouds." Both Lady Gaga and Bradley kept looking to and reaching back to Anthony and Sam, a reflection of their inclusion in the interview. There were no egos; this was family.

When I began interviewing Sam, he had tears in his eyes, and I asked about that. He began to share how after his long career, he had never worked with a level of star as Lady Gaga and gently squeezed her shoulder. She was touched. Sam then said that Bradley had become a real-life brother to him after working on this film. Bradley reached out and grabbed his hand, interlocking his fingers with Sam's. There was love in the room.

"Anthony," I said, "you were telling us before the interview about your high school teacher helping you get into this business. She changed your life." Anthony's face flushed with emotion and tears began streaming down his face.

"I'm from the projects, yo," he strained to say through sobbing.

At this point the entire cast was wiping away tears. Many of the publicists and my producers were crying, but I didn't know until later. All I was doing was trying to hold back my own tears and stay focused on listening to Anthony. He mentioned the kindness of that teacher, and how she had kept him from giving up when he didn't know if he was worthy to dream this dream.

That drama teacher from the Bronx, and the impact of her actions on a young man who was just a part of one of the biggest movies of the year and maybe the decade, was now famous, not by name but by deed. She was powerful enough to have made all of us in the room cry all these years after helping her student. Anthony's story touched us all, because we thought of our own drama teacher, friend, mentor, or boss who went out of their way for us. We relate to being someone who, by all accounts, would not have made it, if it were not for the help of another person who simply believed in us. True kindness supersedes time and distance. It is a superpower that truly connects.

Reciprocity, Imagination, and Empathy

Whenever we interview for a job or a board seat for a foundation or a media opportunity, there are two ways to go about it: it can be an interrogation or a conversation. Interviews for some can be so frequent, they become monotonous. Conversations allow for a friendliness not present in a standard Q&A. Not only do you ask questions of the person across from you, but they start asking you questions. Reciprocity is evidence of shared interest, and interest often comes by empathy, which is imagining what it is like to be in the shoes of the person you are talking to. It leads to much more interesting questions.

Reciprocity, *noun*
1. The practice of exchanging things with others for mutual benefit. . . [9]

Interview, *noun*
A mutual sight or view. . . [10]

I interviewed Ryan Reynolds and his costars Justice Smith and Kathryn Newton in Tokyo to discuss their new movie, *Pokémon Detective Pikachu*. This was one of those epic shoots where we pack as much fun into two or three days as possible—from Ryan and I making sushi, antics at popular tourist attractions, and interviews that culminated on the red carpet. I was so excited to be in

Japan—it was a dream of mine as a kid—and interviewing them for their latest movie about the massively popular Pokémon franchise brought out a childlike giddiness. At the same time, I take every interview seriously. I consciously consider how much money was spent on a movie. I think about all the writing, directing, and production of a screenplay. I put myself in the shoes of the crew and staff and imagine the years these actors have taken to reach the point in their careers where they can lead a film. I think about how intelligent and determined different actors are, and how they hear so many rejections before they get to their big break. I consider how the actors might have had some less-than-fun experiences with interviewers and how many times they get asked the same question, over and over again. There are some questions that you cannot help but ask again because they are crucial to the story of the movie or project. I have learned what is more important is *how* you ask the questions.

I have watched plenty of interviews, and I usually can tell when the interviewer is not invested in the subject matter. For the record, I know when a producer or the person coordinating the interview is not invested either. It becomes a bit of an act at that point, which is truly unfortunate, especially since professional actors can sense bad acting. Many people who have worked in the entertainment industry have taken classes to bring out whatever is on the inside of them, and whatever is on the inside of the audience. After years and years of this, they can be experts on nonverbal communication and body language, and they have been coached to be subtle and to be aware of subtlety.

In a very deliberate, yet delicate way, I initiate conversation at a high level of respect, and they sense that. When I sit down with a celebrity, I see them as an expert or a genius of their craft who has done something very few people will do in their lifetime. All of this is coursing through my mind ahead of every interview, and it is pouring from me in the way that I ask each question. This is empathy, the ability to consider and identify with what someone else could be going through and not to make any judgments.

Funny enough, empathy is what came up in my conversation with Ryan Reynolds while we were making nigiri sushi. The word empathy came up in two or three instances in our interviews. Empathy is what he hopes to teach his children and is something he credits his wife, Blake Lively, with teaching him, especially in difficult relationships. It is also what he thinks of when he is telling jokes.

"I don't ever want to be mean when I am being funny," he said. "If I ever think of a joke that could come off as making fun of someone else, I turn it around on myself. It is still funny, and you can laugh at yourself."

The rest of the cast was in the room at this point and they nodded in agreement. If you google Ryan Reynolds and the word *empathy*, it comes up in over one million results. Maybe empathy is not a word that first comes to mind when you picture the *Deadpool* star with the quick wit, but over the past few years at least, there is evidence that he has made it a mantra and a method for being the best version of himself.

I asked Ryan if he was happy. He said he was, and the reason was because he was doing his life and career in a way that works for him. He discussed how his rise in Hollywood had not been meteoric, and how at one point in his youth he drove a forklift and worked at a grocery store. He spoke of his disappointment after not being able to pursue his dream of doing stand-up comedy—and yet a number of roles he's received over the course of his acting career have honed his style of funny that is now internationally known. He found his sweet spot. I believe first he needed to find empathy.

Imagination is a powerful thing in order to conjure up

empathy. It is also crucial to pursuing your passion in a way that is sustainable. While at the Robot Restaurant, one of Tokyo's extremely popular tourist attractions, Justice, Kathryn, and I continued talking after the interview about pursuing your dreams and living with heart.

"You have to be willing to do what you love, thinking that you are not going to be rewarded for it whatsoever," Justice said. It speaks not only to what you can imagine, but also to the power of imagination to see yourself fulfilled, even while not getting the recognition or success you desire. We talked about how much hard work being in the industry is, giving up time with friends to be there for the early calls, long days, and travel. The actors were not complaining. They were grateful because they had come to a place where they had some sense of knowing how fortunate they were. It did not even seem like a job anymore. That success came in imagining what would happen if they did not get paid; they would still be doing what they loved.

YOUR INTERVIEW WILL MOVE FROM CONVERSATION TO CONNECTION WHEN YOU DESIRE FOR IT TO BE A MUTUAL WIN-WIN.

It made me think about kindness and how, even if we never receive another benefit from being kind, kindness is worth choosing because it is always the right thing. These actors knew their destinies in movie making were right for them, no matter the price they had to pay. I have watched the video of our chat numerous times to remind myself of things that were said that were a real encouragement to me! It was not just about getting a good soundbite.

Kathryn turned to me and asked, "What's your dream?" This was kind of her to ask, and proof that the interview was truly a conversation because she reciprocated by being genuinely interested enough in me as a person to ask a question herself. The hat, so to speak, of the interviewer and interviewee can go away once you truly decide to interact. She later told me that I asked them questions they usually don't get asked during interviews. It was a fun experience, and it was kind of them and their team to not just get the shot with us and leave. We had a great opportunity to have a chat with substance inside that Robot Restaurant!

No matter what kind of interview you are scheduled to have, you will stand out if you do not just go in to perform. Go in with the purpose of making it an enjoyable experience for everyone involved. Your interview will move from conversation to connection when you desire for it to be a mutual win-win.

Making the Most of Your Time in High-Pressure Moments

You cannot slow down the process of interviewing; it requires speed without even the hint of feeling rushed. It is what is needed when closing a deal at the end of the month, for speaking clearly enough to execute an elevator close, and for securing funding for a project approved in a fifteen-minute pitch meeting. This requires savvy and practice. Through working in journalism, I learned a valuable lesson about not letting pressure or time constraints keep you from doing your best to make a great impact.

I will never forget the day I was asked to take no longer than six seconds at the end of my appearance on TV for one of my *World News Tonight* stories. I had to say something simple like, "Police are looking for anyone who might have information to come forward. David." Ideally I would take less time, four to six seconds, as I wrapped up my story and tossed back to anchor David Muir. My

KINDNESS FILLS YOU AND ENVELOPS YOU IN AUTHENTICITY THAT WILL MAKE A GREATER FIRST IMPRESSION IN SECONDS THAN YOU EVER COULD WITHOUT BEING KIND.

father happened to call me right before, and I told him that I was grateful for being on the show but was trying to understand why something that short was worth doing at all. He said, "Adrienne, it only takes a second to make an impact."

It took all the pressure about time off me, and now I know I can get a lot across in seconds! Think of the world we live in now—it is all about mere seconds of video on various platforms. Boomerang videos alone have the same action repeated in a loop and captivate people every day! Using viral videos on social media as proof, I know that in one second, I can look at the person I am interviewing in the eye and convey love, kindness, and respect. Similarly to how we can read a room, as I said earlier, it is important to know that other people are getting a read on you. In a moment, they will know if you are the real deal. Kindness fills you and envelops you in authenticity that will make a greater first impression in seconds than you ever could without being kind.

Stories of Kindness

Kindness in you will attract and bring out the kindness of others. In an interview with actor Nathan Fillion, I began the conversation asking about his long career and how funny he was. I saved a question for the end, asking what he would consider one of the most important lessons he has learned in his twenty-five-plus-year career.

"My mother got me this little book and she would write sound, sage advice on every page," he said. "One of the things she wrote was, 'Be kind to people on the way up because those are the same people you'll meet on the way down.' That kindness has always served me well."

After he left one of the photographers remarked, "A scholar and a gentleman. He was great."

"Right!?" I said.

Our sound guy, Brian spoke up. "I remember when we interviewed Queen Latifah. I was getting her microphone on and I had found out she loved bikes. And I am really into bikes too. So as I was putting the mic on, I asked her about that. You should have seen her face." He scrunched up his face and looked up with his eyes to mimic the way she looked up at him when he said it. "She became so comfortable and loose after that. It was awesome."

"Kudos to you for doing research on a guest when you didn't have to. That was very thoughtful of you!" I replied.

Kind is doing things that are right, no matter your job description. I am sure the interviewer had a better chat with Queen Latifah after being warmed up with the audio engineer's chat about bikes. It all helps.

"You know, it reminds me of Hugh Jackman," the photographer said. "One of the guys on the crew had mentioned it was our sound guy Ken's birthday and somehow Hugh overheard as he was about to walk in. As the producer was directing him to his seat, Hugh looks around and said, 'I want to say happy birthday to Ken! Happy birthday!' He went over and gave him a big hug. It was so cool."

Several weeks later, Hugh Jackman was a guest on our show. I had never met him before, but I had every confidence I could walk into his green room and tell him about all the kind things he had become known for. I told him the story of the birthday hug. It certainly surprised him for a moment, and he listened intently.

I've learned that kindness makes you comfortable, bold, and willing to do things with purpose that would otherwise make many people nervous.

"You know, as a kid, my mum would tell me to always lead with kindness. I guess I have held onto that one," he replied. "Thank you so much for telling me that story. It was so nice to meet you."

Kindness gives you an internal barometer of good. You just know when it's right. Kindness makes you confident without second-guessing.

One day between shows, I turned the corner and there was Garth Brooks strumming his guitar. I took out my camera and said, "Hey, this should be on Instagram! Garth Brooks is in the hallway! Will you sing us something?"

I hadn't planned on singing, but since I had requested a song I knew all the words to, he obliged me with a duet! That was truly kind. After the once-in-a-lifetime sing-along, I screamed, "I just sang with Garth Brooks!" I was so impressed that he would make the time. He was so chill, I didn't think twice about asking him for the video. I think Garth saw it as I did—just a moment to have fun. Afterward, one of my producers called to tell me that Garth was requesting the video. He posted it on Facebook to his legions of fans with a personal message to me, which was special! I could never have guessed this was going to happen, but it was awesome.

Kindness brings good surprises.

Kobe

I had the pleasure of interviewing Kobe Bryant about writing his first book, which he said was more fulfilling than the game of basketball. He had won an Oscar for his animated short *Dear*

Basketball, and it was time for a new passion for the superstar. After a twenty-year NBA career, where he admitted he had often been strictly business and all about scoring, the proud family man and father had taken time to reflect. I asked him what one of his biggest lessons in his career was.

"I think the most important lesson was a lesson of self-acceptance. Ultimately a lesson in compassion, to say, you know, I don't know what you went through, but I know you went through something, and I see you. And so it's a lesson in empathy that I certainly wish I had at an earlier age."

He continued: "We learn there's more to the game than just the game, right? And being able to be present and listen to your teammates and what it is that they may be experiencing in their daily lives and how that may affect their behavior and their performance on the court and just being there for them."

Get a Room

One of my favorite moments of kindness at work did not involve an interview, but a moment in the hair and makeup room. Barbara Corcoran of ABC's *Shark Tank* had come to our weekend show. She had a hair and makeup team accompany her, but it was revealed she didn't know where she was going to get dressed. As I sat in my chair listening, I thought, *We don't have a room for her? She can use my room.* For a moment, I hesitated because I did not want to be abrupt after overhearing the conversation. Soon, I just couldn't contain myself.

"You can use my room," I said. "It's on the fourth floor. I will show your hairstylist where it is and you can get dressed and have a moment of quiet. Take your time to prepare, whatever you need; just make yourself at home."

I could tell she was visibly relieved. Anyone who has to wake up before 6:00 a.m., look bright-eyed, and be TV-ready needs a little more care and quiet time first. Right before she came up, I made sure to tidy up a bit, and I left a note card expressing our thanks to her for coming. Kindness doesn't try to impress, but it is impressive.

KINDNESS DOESN'T TRY TO IMPRESS, BUT IT IS IMPRESSIVE.

I did not talk to Barbara again until after her interview, when she came to the set and gave me a big hug. "I want a picture with you," she said, as she thanked me again for the gesture. Later, when I went back to my office, she had written on the envelope I had placed her thank-you card in, "Your mom did a great job with you!" She doodled a flower alongside her note.

Not having a proper dressing room could have been a disappointing experience for Barbara. There are so many distractions from day to day, and kindness helps us keep a good sense of humor and does not take anything, including ourselves, too seriously. Once I accidently threw my phone across the room, on camera, while asking questions. We all had a good laugh. I remember during one interview the elevator was so loud it nearly shook the building. Instead of pretending no one else heard it, I was honest and said to the guest, "Listen, forgive us for the sound of that elevator. It's really loud but we are going to have a nice chat anyway." Kindness is honest and breaks tension.

I hope what you will take away from this chapter so far is that, while we all have a different style of doing our jobs, we can all incorporate kindness. Whether you are an attorney, pastry chef, or construction worker, when doing your job, decide that whomever is across from you, you can imagine being in their shoes and seeing them for who they really are.

When I go into an interview, I see it as a time to do at least these three things for sure:

1. I want to honor the person I'm interviewing with equality and fairness in an environment of kindness that allows for them to feel safe, appreciated, and free to be themselves.
2. I want to ask questions that inspire and open them up to think.
3. I want all of us, those on camera and off, to be inspired and better for having had the interview.

These objectives can be applied to interactions with friends, family, and new connections.

Kindness to Yourself

There are great lessons we can learn from work about ourselves. When I interviewed the cast of the movie *Widows*, starring an ensemble of women led by Viola Davis, the women shared how their favorite part of working on the film was that the director, Steve McQueen, helped them discover parts of themselves they had either not portrayed before or kept hidden. His compassion made them extremely loyal to the project. When I asked them about what they learned that was applicable to life, actress Elizabeth Debicki said, "Be kind to yourself—as you see who you are."

She proceeded to tell a story about a scene in the movie where she began slouching because her six-foot, three-inch frame was often taller than her male counterpart. At one point she said McQueen stepped in and told Debicki to stand up straight and stop slouching.

"He would tell me to own it," she said.

We could all afford to be kinder to ourselves as we own who we really are, especially as we are in growth spurts or learning a new skill. We need to be gentle with ourselves as we accept what we cannot change and admit what needs to be eliminated that is hindering authentic and fearless expression. In the process of activating kindness, you may end up doing something unkind. If you ever hear yourself saying, "I am not kind enough," it is because you have forgotten who you are for a moment and are trying to feel bad. What you are saying is, "I am not enough." You may have raised your voice with others, but prior to that you may have whispered to yourself constantly that you were not good enough. Saying what is untrue about ourselves is our internal way of inflicting punishment.

Self-bullying makes us try hard to do everything perfectly. Those who beat themselves up think they have to be unrealistically good or better than other people in order to be loved or appreciated. Self-doubt can act as a bully, with infiltrating thoughts that say, *You're fake* or *You're not ready*. It becomes easier to believe those attacking voices when facing a challenge or a new project and looking for any excuse to get out of it for fear of rejection.

Accepting who we are prevents us from being the walking wounded, smiling on the outside while messed up on the inside. It makes us strong enough to brush off insults, the lack of appreciation, or "borrowed" ideas you did not get the credit for. Self-acceptance can nullify the hateful words and actions of others that would otherwise last in our memory for years. Negativity, anger, and fear do not have the power to interrupt who we are when we are *convinced* we are kind.

Brad Pitt and I talked about how he brings a little bit of himself to each character. He packages an emotion from his own life into the scene in order to evoke the right tone for the role he is playing. I asked him if he ever left the scene carrying the same emotions he had conjured up, be that anger, depression, or regret.

"Oh no," he said with a dimpled grin. "I just shake it off. Once I am done with that scene, I get up and I am not even thinking about those feelings anymore. I just shake it off. In fact, I am usually on to the next movie or what I am going to eat for dinner. It's in the past."

Whatever feelings we have that do not line up with the truth of who we are have to be shaken off. Never say anything to yourself or about yourself that you would not say to a best friend. It also helps to create kindness affirmations. I've met and heard about celebrities making clearly defined goals for what they will be known for. "I will be on national television," "I will win a Grammy Award," or "I will make the Forbes list," is as easy to say as, "I am kind." What I do is not who I am. Who I am influences and infuses everything I do. Telling yourself that you are kind lays a foundation for anything else you decide to embark on because it is a statement that you love yourself. Loving yourself establishes a firm footing. More than anything else, it is important to know that we are loved and to love ourselves. We have the power to craft our world and to declare our truth. I get to architect the person I am.

"I am kind" is a statement that defies the gravity of abuse, conflict, or your past behavior. "I am kind" is a choice that, in light of mistakes, poverty, or hard knocks, ensures these truths remain: "I am loved. I love myself. I forgive myself."

CHAPTER 7

POWER TO OPEN DOORS

There are people we believe we should be kind to. Being kind to everyone else leads to spontaneous adventure and unexpected opportunity.

I've learned that opportunity is a door with a kind person on the other side of the lock who smiles and says, "Welcome." The key I've found to those doors that appear locked, the key that no one can steal from you, is to be kind. If we try to open the door with charm, our appeals to the keeper of the door may backfire. We might say the wrong thing, or they might be unimpressed with our wit and feigned interest in them because they know we only want to talk to them for what they can do for us. Some have tried to rush the door of opportunity and kick it in with sheer grit and willpower. Typically, though, that is liable to hurt someone. Plus, it can appear coarse and rude.

Kindness gives you the proper balance of humility and confidence instead of being so eager to coerce the gatekeepers—be they managers, influencers, owners, or administrators. It is important to keep in mind that they are not the only ones who have something treasured. Most opportunity seekers feel there is a chase, a hunt for who to talk to, and what that person and possibility could do for them. When you assert yourself in life with genuine kindness, you are acknowledging that the treasure is inside of you and so is the map. You know that wherever you go, no matter what doors open, you are a valuable commodity and an asset to any group of people. You're also rightly convinced that most gatekeepers recognize true kindness. I never diminish the fact that someone in a position of power has the ability to open the door for me. I just refuse to diminish my own power to be a solution for the one at the door. My kindness is what sets me apart. I express to whoever has an opportunity for me that I, too, have something they want and need. I believe it, and I say it all the time, that I am here to bring peace, answers, and my unique abilities to every situation. I truly believe that each one of us can do this when we are genuinely kind.

A practical example of this is by fulfilling your kindest potential when you speak to your boss. You're not nervous, trying to impress them and hoping they will help you out or give you advice. Instead, you go to be a gift and listen to find out if there's anything you can do to solve a problem. It might be as simple as checking in with them just to see how they are doing. You may learn they need more volunteers for their annual day of giving, and you sign up. You just might come up with an innovative cost-cutting measure by listening to your boss with kindness. When you are invited to a holiday party or fundraiser, it's not for the free meal or to even concern yourself with who you might meet.

You go to these events, the grocery store, or out on a date *as an investor*. It doesn't mean you are everyone's solution; it means you are open to it. This doesn't take the fun out of life; it makes life much more exciting and interesting! When you are on a mission not to get but to give, you put yourself in position to walk through open doors. You are open to the fact that, yes, you ran out of almond milk, and the checkout clerk, or someone in line, or the manager, or a stranger on the way there might just need a solution with your name on it.

We've got to start realizing that those little necessities in life give us the opportunity to do the real living, by taking us on an unexpected journey. I might smile at someone, and it makes their day brighter. I might find out about my dry cleaner's mother being in the hospital and encourage them while picking up my clothing. It might be that I find out my neighbor is a talented photographer, and my sister needs new headshots, so I make the introduction. It becomes practical and organic and, soon, you'll do it daily in the moments in between errands and the evening commute home. You'll value yourself with that treasure inside of you and won't just put in your earbuds and walk out the door. Your new soundtrack will be conversations with the people you want to help and those you didn't even notice before. In turn, you'll notice people, and those you've never met before will start to come to you with a kind introduction and then ideas and maybe a golden opportunity.

One of my most memorable open-door moments came when the door had already been shut once. At one point in my television journey, I had a big opportunity presented to me that was a dream come true. It was a new job, everything I had been hoping for, and things moved quickly. In a matter of days, everything around me would change, in a new city. When I was offered the position and received a call from one of the closest people in my life, we laughed and cried and celebrated it all happening. Then the crash. As I attempted to walk through this newly opened door, I tripped over the negotiation phase. This was before I had an agent, and the deal I was attempting to work out fell through. I was, for the first time in my career, out of work with no backup plan. When things didn't happen the way I expected, I was in a hard place. I had extreme pressure to give up on myself. I started questioning my entire purpose. If it were not for the persistent kindness of my life coach, I would still be under the blankets. He told me, "Go to work, even if you have to go flip burgers." At the time it felt irrational and cruel, but he would not let me give up. This would mean moving to a city with no friends, no contacts, and no money. Sometimes you will have to do things that make *no sense* to be in position for the largest open doors.

Traveling on my own, I set up a meeting with the woman who had been negotiating with me, and she agreed to meet for coffee. This was a huge kindness on her part. There are so many people who wish they could sit down with someone like this. I truly will never forget this moment. She told me they had filled the position. Now, they didn't have any work available for me, but she said they would call me if something came up.

They ended up calling me in as a freelancer for a couple of days a week but couldn't guarantee me any consistent hours. My confidence was nearly devastated, and I finally started interviewing at local restaurants so I wouldn't starve. The first place I went to was right by my house, a burger joint. The manager had only seen me as a customer by this point. When I asked for work, he looked stunned. "I've never had a journalist ask me to work as a waitress," he said.

I remember telling him it was "respectable work" before going home and crying my eyes out. Suffice it to say, he had just hired some waitstaff and didn't have any open positions.

I was hired on my birthday, at a different place, just down the street from the job I had lost, as a restaurant hostess. Filling out the application to work for minimum wage—with the reminder that I was entering another year of my life farther from the goals I had set for myself—was another moment that brought me to tears. I did not let anyone I worked with or mentored know all that I was going through. It was too hard to explain at this point. I simply soldiered on like all I did was television, though instead of sitting next to my future co-anchors at a news desk, I was seating them for lunch.

Only a few people knew how intense this roller coaster was. They are to this day the dearest people to me. Without their kind phone calls, I might not be here. While I knew it was only temporary, working between the two gigs was an out-of-body experience. On rough days, I would think back on what I'd left behind to pursue my dream—stability, a constant paycheck, a nice home. I was miserable and guarded, but I had a brave face.

So many mistakes had caused me to question myself, but the one thing about being kind is that it does not waver with a lack of confidence. I was extremely vulnerable and insecure on the one hand, because I did not know how everything would work out. I only knew to keep being kind and doing a good job. Keep smiling at customers. Keep calm when we hit the lunch or dinner rush. Keep saying hello to the servers and bussers and looking them in the eye. Little did my fellow employees know that I would sometimes have to duck into the coat closet while giving myself a pep talk: *"The kind of work you do and the circumstances you are in do not define you! You know who you are, no matter where you work, no matter what you are doing now!"*

One reason the restaurant business is among one of the most intense industries on the planet is because you are in close proximity with so many different personalities while getting the business of the day done. I soon implemented something I learned from my media career—to intentionally bring peace and compliment people so that they feel respected and appreciated. Kindness is capable of making up the difference when you don't feel as capable emotionally due to stress.

Only a few days into working at the restaurant, a name popped up on the computer screen; it was that same woman I had met for coffee and spoken to in the failed negotiations. She was coming in for a 12:30 lunch, and I would be one of the first faces she would see. I was concerned she would question why I was there. I refused to be ashamed or nervous, but I did feel my heart rate go up. Things around me could point to my career being sidelined, but the dream made me unrealistically certain that it was worth doing whatever it took. Kindness helped me to stand up straight and put a smile on my face when everything else in me wanted to crawl into that coat closet again.

"What are you doing here!" she exclaimed. (Which is exactly what I imagined she'd say.)

"Well, I am a host on TV and I am host here, so let me show you to your table. Follow me," I said with enthusiasm as I motioned her to her seat.

She looked at me in awe.

"You know, I have some ideas for you I've been thinking about," she said. "I'll call you a little later this week."

I nodded and left her to enjoy her lunch. Within two weeks I was presented a media contract and quit working at the restaurant. Again, this boss of the television world was kind enough to *reopen* the door. She had a long line of people waiting and hoping to get on her calendar. Because I didn't quit, I was in a position to be the recipient of her kindness. We give up sometimes because we think it's too late or believe that no one has our back. We do not consider that someone else is kind enough to hold the door open for us a second or third time. If you know you belong inside an opportunity, start believing that other people know you belong as well. A huge part of kindness is knowing that other people will be kind to you. Kindness is as much about being kind as it is about increasing your expectations to receive kindness.

On a Plane

One reason I enjoy my job so much is that I get to travel. For years I wondered if I would ever get to achieve my dream of traveling all around the world. Being a journalist at the network level afforded me that opportunity. Most people desire an adventure, traveling to exotic and unusual locations, tasting amazing food, and experiencing new and interesting people. For me, the unexpected friendships with strangers and meeting interesting people is the best part of an adventure. I find that kindness shown to the people on these paths can open doors that others might have trouble finding.

On one cross-country flight, I sat next to a woman who looked like she had just come from the wilderness. She was dressed for the outdoors, her face was flushed, and she was wearing stacks of colorful handmade bracelets on her wrists. I was curious about her story. I could tell she was physically exhausted. She was on the phone and didn't seem to want to be bothered. I started flipping through my *American Way* magazine and, at one point, I looked over, made eye contact, and offered a kind smile.

Somehow, we struck up a conversation. It turns out she had been traveling over three continents, and Africa had been just one stop. She had been bitten all over by some kind of bug on one of her journeys, which explained the discomfort I sensed. Her next trip would be a visit with a group who had an audience with Pope Francis. Only after chatting with her did I discover she was an international business owner, philanthropist, and change agent for some global causes. I would not have met such a successful and interesting woman had I not first offered a smile and then been kind enough to engage someone who looked like she didn't want to be bothered. As we exited the plane, she looked at me and said, "I never talk to anyone on planes, but this was a pleasant surprise."

OPENNESS IS INITIATED BY A KIND ACT.

I kept in touch with her through email and, several months later, coordinated a time that she and I could meet over tea when she was in New York City. She recommended I see the movie *Free Solo*, she shared how she became a CEO, and she talked about her passion projects. I remember asking her about how she met her husband and how she knew what her calling was in life. She was a compelling storyteller, sharing openly about pain and loss and her soul mate. If she was afraid of anything, she would play that fear out in a worst-case scenario. She explained that once she saw the potential outcome, she wasn't afraid anymore. She humbly and candidly shared her life as a woman who had dared boldly and with an appreciation for risk. I was inspired by her, and it all started with a conversation that wouldn't have happened if I wasn't open to it. Openness is initiated by a kind act.

Open Doors

You hear a lot of people talk about the power of positivity, the power of attraction. I'm not denying their existence at all—but it can be a rather abstract construct until we see how to practically apply that power to our lives. If you intentionally adopt and exude kindness, delivering eye contact and a genuine smile when someone enters a room, you will notice more people will stop and ask you for directions, ask to join your table, and think of you for opportunities. I want you to think of your own open doors as you read this example, and how one door leads to another because of kindness.

Open Door #1: A time to shine. A fellow correspondent of mine needed someone to fill in for her as emcee of a national organization's annual fundraiser. She told me she called because she believed I could be discerning and sensitive toward the cause.

"Sure," I said, honored that she would consider me to be her substitute. I scheduled a call with the organizers of the group, excited to be a part of what seemed like an impactful event. However, I was unfamiliar with the organization. The last thing I wanted to do was come off as "just filling in." I could tell the organizer was a little bit concerned herself, especially with the fundraiser now only two days away.

"Don't worry," I assured her, "I've emceed hundreds of events, and I will make sure to get there early enough that we can go over the program in person. This will be great."

I wanted to give her optimism in a time of great pressure for her and her organization. The event was a success, and it was only the tip of the iceberg. I want to show you the many things that came out of me saying yes to a coworker who needed a substitute at this event.

Open Door #2: The opportunity to shine a light on others. We are constantly presented with ways to open doors for others. One of the women I was going to recognize at this event was from my hometown. She worked for an airline in the airport I flew into every month. I thought, *Perfect, I will tie in a sentiment about coming home.*

Though at the podium, I ended up going off script to call that woman up. Why? Because I realized her story of helping save two girls from being kidnapped was much more compelling than my ability to tap dance between portions of the program. She was amazing and so comfortable on camera you would have thought we rehearsed it. It ended up being one of the highlights of the evening.

Open Door #3: Reconnection with an industry ally. Between my emcee duties and the evening raffle, I discovered one of our long-standing producers at ABC was in the audience. She and I had met in an elevator once. In that forty-five seconds between floors, I introduced myself because of her bright smile. She emailed me right away and kindly invited me to coffee, but our schedules never aligned. That night we made a clearer connection, and one of her friends joined us for dinner.

Open Door #4: New friendships that are a win-win. That friend stayed in touch and invited me to do some speaking for her at future women's events. She also invited me to a holiday party; we had a great time to connect in the hour-long car ride, where we were able to share similar interests. We ended up partnering together for some business that benefits both of our long-range goals.

Open Door #5: The hero I honored ended up connecting me to a vital contact to help a loved one. Three months later, I had a friend who needed some travel help. It was a bit complicated, so I reached out to the woman I met who worked for the airline.

She couldn't help me then but introduced me to a colleague who could. The woman who helped me has become not only an asset, but also a friend who has helped me help others during emergencies and seemingly impossible situations.

When you are kind it creates a ripple effect. A habit that has helped me is being able to take time to reflect on all of the doors that opened as a result of one act of kindness, one time of saying yes.

People who are meeting you for the first time will notice your kindness and be pleasantly surprised, which creates a tangible openness from the onset. There is also the open door from the practice of being kind. Becoming known for being kind will set you up for rising to the top of the list for opportunities. I was talking to the news director of a major media company. I brought up one of his reporters, Miriam Hernandez. There were quite a few people who I knew inside the company, but I wanted to find her first to tell her thank you. When I made a move from local to network news, she'd called and left me the most touching voice mail. I still have it saved on my phone from years ago. The news director told me: "Miriam is great. She is not only the sweetest person but she's just so good at what she does. I believe she is one of the best, most compassionate reporters we have in the building. We love her. She can work here as long as she wants."

At a time when careers are at times less predictable, and tenure at a company is shorter, this woman was being promised lifetime job security! A knowledge of your reputation for kindness among those who know you and those who have the power of influence and decision once they see or hear of your reputation, will open the door for priceless adventures and spontaneous surprises that might otherwise be overlooked.

Take the time today to consider the times in your life when

you were kind and someone noticed or remembered you for a great opportunity because of your track record or first impression.

Here are some things to remember:

- Make eye contact and offer a willing smile to anyone. Give yourself a tech break when you go out to pick up dinner or dry cleaning. Look kindly at others. Be open to striking up conversation with those you've never met.
- Be willing to walk through doors you didn't open. Success stories are not all the hard work and hustle. Many are where they are today because of the kindness of someone who just gave them a shot.
- Be willing to be a replacement player in a time of need. When someone asks you to step into their place, it could be an opportunity in disguise.

CHAPTER 8

YES, NEW FRIENDS

Friendliness empowers us to architect and cultivate deeper, more fulfilling relationships in every area.

Being friendly is a form of kindness that maintains current relationships and keeps us more aware of all people. Not everyone is going to be your friend, but you can be friendly to everyone. I list these definitions to make a clear word picture. *Kindness* is defined as "having or showing a friendly, generous, and considerate nature."[11] By being patient, respectful, and a good listener to those you know and those you don't know, you're being kind. You've experienced this from people you meet one time and it feels like you've known forever, and those who seem to have never met a stranger. These are the people who are often called "a breath of fresh air." Everyone has their own style, and you will grow and develop this like a muscle. Here is one practical way to be friendly and create a lasting memory that will feed constant hope into your soul: *Thank the people you see doing good!*

When I see someone doing something generous or kind, I will often go out of my way to tell the person, "I saw you help them; that was very kind of you. Please keep doing what you're doing. You make a difference."

I once witnessed a younger man open the door for an elderly person. It put a huge smile on my face, then suddenly I was compelled to turn around and catch up with that man, who was now walking in the opposite direction. "Excuse me!" I shouted as I began walking faster. "Thank you for holding that door for that man. That was very kind and it was awesome to see!"

Now I wasn't the only one smiling. I could tell that thank you made a difference in his day. May he never forget that someone was paying attention to his good deed.

Fast Friends

Being friendly to those you might call strangers happens organically, if we stay open. You begin by choosing to be friendly. That decision will fuel you helping others in simple ways and noticing the helpers. When you see someone doing something good or heroic, remark on how special it is and commend them. It's the one sure way to spawn more heroic action. I make these fast friends everywhere I go, and you can too. If we allow it, we are all on a bigger mission, as if we were destined to be in that same place at the same time. It makes for some truly remarkable moments and pleasant surprises. By treating everyone as friends—including the people you will likely never see again—you get to witness some of the most spontaneous and brightest moments of humanity.

While walking through New York City one afternoon, in a bit of a hurry with a member of my team, I saw a black man in a baseball cap with his arm around this older white man, supporting the weight of his body as he helped him get into a cab. The taxi driver was standing outside the vehicle waiting patiently in the right lane of a busy street while other cars and tons of people tried to navigate around them. I was captivated by the sight of two men moving slowly in the midst of a hectic scene. I asked a guy standing on the corner if he saw what happened.

BY TREATING EVERYONE—INCLUDING THE PEOPLE YOU WILL LIKELY NEVER SEE AGAIN—AS FRIENDS, YOU GET TO WITNESS SOME OF THE MOST SPONTANEOUS AND BRIGHTEST MOMENTS OF HUMANITY.

"Oh, the old guy fell pretty hard. It was sad. Then the dude helped him up and helped him get a cab."

I swung around and the cab was rolling out with the older man safely inside. That helper was already on the move, walking quickly down the street. I turned to my colleague.

"I feel like I need to tell him thank you for doing that. Will you come with me?"

He agreed as we chased the guy down. "Excuse me!" As I finally got his attention he turned and stopped. "What happened with the older gentleman? You helped him?"

"Anyone would have done the same thing," he said. "I mean I would expect to do something like that for anyone, but this grandfather, he fell pretty hard; he was disoriented. I made sure the cab driver knew where he wanted to go. He'll be all right. I was just on my way to work. I'm a little late now, but he'll be all right."

I thanked him for doing the right thing and let him know that it was so awesome that he helped that man instead of just walking by. He was humble. As he left, I realized I was looking at a picture of a good Samaritan. It's a description of what we are all called to be in life: fast friends. Fast friends aren't just nice. Fast friends:

- Pay attention and are situationally aware.
- Do whatever is needed in the moment.
- Are quick to acknowledge others around them with action, eye contact, a smile, or another affirming gesture.
- Don't get caught up in what others may think of them in the moment, they are more concerned with the need.
- Remember to treat those they'll likely never see again with care.

The first rebuttal I would hear from anyone is that they couldn't possibly see how they'd have the time to initiate this kind of connection regularly. It happens by starting where you are—work, home, life.

There are times in life when, if we step back, we realize we haven't been friendly to our friends! When was the last time you called your buddy when you didn't need something? Friends are the ones we choose, we know their quirks and flaws and we still love them anyway. We can treat our family the same way. Write an encouraging note and slip it in the mail or call just to say hi to your sister.

We can also start being better to what I call our "captive

audience." Captive audiences are those people in places where we might not have cell service. We can strike up a conversation in a checkout line or while waiting at jury duty or the DMV. You're already there together; why not give your phone a break and connect with those around you?

Don't try too hard. Compliment the person standing beside you or give a word to inspire someone or make them smile. The other night while out of town I went to dinner and ordered the biggest piece of the restaurant's world-famous coconut cake. I cut a piece off and boxed the rest. I brought it to the front desk of my hotel and asked if anyone would like a piece. They were truly grateful. It's something I would have done for a friend.

One of my favorite things that people I do not know do for me when I'm on a plane is help me put my bag up or take it down from the overhead bin. I remember when I was in London as a college student, and I had no idea what I was doing with a seventy-pound bag at the train station. It was almost impossible to move on my own, and someone just came up and helped me get it up the steps and onto the train. Another time in Manhattan, I had just unloaded two seventy-pound bags from a cab and was looking to meet someone at their job. A woman came up to me smiling and said, "Let me help you." She grabbed one of the bags and rolled it into the building I was headed to without being asked. I hurried to keep up with her. She was gone before I had a chance to say thank you, as she was headed off to work. Kindness comes just when we need it.

KINDNESS COMES JUST WHEN WE NEED IT.

When I see parents at a store who have a child who is having a moment, often times I'll be walking by and I'll ask the child, "Are you listening to your mom? I know she loves you very much." The mom or dad is at first surprised, and then smiles.

They don't mind a brief diversion from the meltdown, and a lot of times the child stops crying because of the surprise of someone talking to them who isn't their parent! Once in a restaurant, a friend and I made sure to say to two parents with three very active children covered in waffles and egg, "You guys are amazing. You have your hands full. It's the best job you'll ever have, and your family is beautiful." I have found parents are very appreciative when someone notices how much of a gift and a challenge it is to spend quality family time.

Another time, a nanny was unloading two children out of a New York City bus right in front of me as I was seated outside Lincoln Center. One of them, a girl around four or five, was holding the hand of her sitter, while the second, who I'm guessing was no older than two, was screaming his head off.

I directed my attention to the little boy from my bench, with every intention of trying to get the kid to calm down and help the sitter. "Hey! There's no crying in baseball! You're okay!" The sitter was surprised, which I expected. What I didn't expect was the girl to begin a conversation with me.

"He always does that," she said.

"Maybe he just needs a nap?" I replied.

"Yeah," she said. "You should get tickets to the ballet here. It's very good," she said, motioning to Lincoln Center as the trio walked off.

I laughed inside. When they were still walking down the sidewalk, and I was smiling at the thought of a preschooler giving me an idea for my social calendar, I sensed someone was looking at me. I looked up and the little girl, still walking away, had her gaze directly on me. I waved. She waved back. Another thirty seconds and she looked back to see if I was still there, we exchanged another wave. Children need to see positive expressions of friendliness in the world.

One thing you can do to invite these types of kindness interactions is sit outside in a park or an open plaza and just be. One day, I was reading and eating my lunch, and an older woman came and asked if she could sit at my table. I obliged her. She proceeded to tell me about the history of the Upper West Side of Manhattan, and how at one point she would never have walked out her front door. We made small talk, and after about twenty minutes, she thanked me and left to meet friends for dinner.

I've done this many times at private clubs and outside busy cafes. People are pleasantly surprised when they see a kind face. The point is not to become besties with everyone you meet or to invade anyone's personal space. The key is to be like a safe harbor in a sea of busy people too distracted to notice. It only takes one harsh word or one uncaring glance to make it a bad day for someone. But when we reflect on our good days, we recognize that it's those little moments when some unnamed person bought our coffee, held the door for us, or allowed us to cut in the security line at the airport—as well as the smiles from a half dozen people at work—that made the day better.

I remember being out to dinner with one of my former bosses. We ordered so much food! When the time came for the bill to be paid, the server informed my boss that someone had purchased our meal. He was shocked. "I need to take you to dinner more often!" he said. It is a great feeling to know someone noticed you and decided to do something kind. To this day I have no idea who paid. I had a big smile on my face because I wasn't as surprised as my boss. I know people who often anonymously buy meals in restaurants for those they don't know. I have done it myself for the sweet couple who looked like they were celebrating an anniversary or the parents taking their daughters to a birthday lunch. Another way to do this is to buy groceries for the person in line ahead or behind you. Once I was in line at a deli and a police officer was behind me. Before he could notice I asked if the cashier would ring up his meal with mine. It feels great to be a "secret Santa" all year long.

While most of these interactions are brief, I always allow for them to develop into something more. I checked into a hotel in Dallas for one night on a work trip and came to the counter around 11:30 p.m. I was spent and didn't feel my best. I was doing my utmost to stay energetic and upbeat so that I didn't come off rude.

"Good evening," the desk agent said, with hardly any eye contact.

It wasn't that she wasn't pleasant, but she wasn't warm and friendly. I thought, *Maybe she doesn't feel her best now either.* Instead of getting irritated, I just remained quiet.

She went over the details in my itinerary, and when she asked about my corporate account I said, "Yes, I work for Disney."

"Oh?" It was like a light turned on for her. "How is it working for them?"

I could tell she was likely weary of working at a hotel, albeit a nice one, and she had other passions. If you read between the lines of what people are saying and practice hearing what they are *really* saying, you can help them more effectively.

"I'll tell you, I've dreamed of being where I am today," I said. "I just went to Disney World and the slogan at the gate of the park reads 'Where Dreams Come True.' I know that you work hard, and it can go different than you planned, but it's all worth it to do what you said you wanted to do. I know you have a dream bigger than where you currently are. If you need some advice, feel free to connect over Instagram. Here's my card."

She was almost in tears. I realized she was looking at me eye-to-eye now.

"Wow. Thank you so much," she said. "I really love everything Disney and, you're right, I do want to do more than this. I'm just starting, but what you just said was really encouraging. Thank you. You're going to make me cry."

When you have a lifestyle of being a friend to all, you build a discernment that will make you more and more of a specialist at helping others. You see, being friendly isn't just a moment of pleasantries. When you have a lifestyle of being a friend to all, you build a discernment that will make you more and more of a specialist at helping others. You'll go deeper than a gesture when you least expect it. You'll be able to address someone's real issue. You'll not only see needs; you'll see people for who they really are. And you might help make someone's dream come true.

Being friendly with everyone opens you up to new opportunities to impact other people's lives. As discussed in this section, here are some ideas for reaching out:

Allow a coworker to just talk. We all just need to express ourselves sometimes! As you are kinder, you'll be more sensitive to others and what they need, even if that means you have to slow down for a few minutes. They might be going through something at home or on the job. This is time for them to pour out their hearts. Maybe you give advice or just listen.

Care about people even against a deadline. When you have an appointment, consider more than just the task at hand. Be sensitive as to whether they might need a friendly chat or coffee break once the job is done. Create moments that allow people to decompress whenever possible, in the midst of full schedules.

Be a friend to your managers, mentees, or mentors. There are people in your office and industry that you have received emails from for years and never met! Let's not just check people off the list. Get to know them! Ask for five minutes and see how it blossoms. Listen more than you talk, especially during those first few conversations. The goal is to get to know them.

Check in on a friend, former customer, or family member "just because." Forget about old history, the last time you called, or what they did (or you did) that you didn't like. Just reach out and treat them like you would a dear friend, with a true concern for their life and what concerns them in this moment.

Get to know the person next to you at the nail salon. Remember those places where there is a captive audience! This is one of the few places we can unplug, as texting and calling is hindered by that manicure. Strike up a conversation and see if the customer next to you is someone you can make the day brighter for.

Chat up the person you just asked for directions. Whether walking in the same direction as someone on the street, shopping in the produce aisle, or standing at the streetlight, just strike up a conversation. Some would call it bold and others would call it serendipitous. Flow and feel it out.

Being friendly gives credence to our interconnectedness. (It's a good way to get outside your box!) It is intentional when you are not just in your own head or to-do list like a robot. Smile at people as you wait in line at the restaurant host stand or movie theater box office. These are all ways that make you feel more alive.

Building an Inner Circle

Having friends keeps you healthy. Whether you are outgoing or admittedly shy, no one on the planet benefits from always being alone. The former US surgeon general defined loneliness as an epidemic, equivalent to smoking fifteen cigarettes a day, reducing lifespan, and feelings of isolation at work, and tied addiction to a lack of social connection.[12]

In the UK, then prime minister Theresa May appointed a Minister of Loneliness to address the issue of people who feel unloved and have no one to talk to. According to a 2017 report on loneliness, published by the Jo Cox Commission, more than nine million people in Britain often or always feel lonely.[13]

Isolation can devastate us and blind us to others in the world who need someone to notice them. I am convinced that if we were to take every one of the loneliest people and give them the means and a mission to go out and help someone else, it would begin to heal their relational wounds. And having that purpose would create a paradigm shift in the way they see the world. When you keep to yourself, it's possible you've lost hope. Many have baggage surrounding friendship.

Even the word *friends* can elicit all kinds of responses from every one of us. When you think of that word, your immediate reaction could be a big, broad smile as a warm, fuzzy feeling washes over you and your latest memory of your bestie pops into your head. You could feel sadness or regret over the loss of a friend, the dissolution of a friendship, or a hurt from a friend who betrayed you. You might feel like you don't have any true friends and immediately feel shame or frustration. No matter the pain of the past, or the hurdles you face in forging new relationships, the way to being a friend is being friendly.

I myself have had times in life where I didn't want to let people in, and being a friend to people who simply were not friendly was a challenge. We have all had disappointments and hurts in life; it's natural to want to protect ourselves or to prevent ourselves from ever being hurt again. But deciding not to get to know people puts us in an emotional prison. After I made the choice to treat everyone as a friend, I became a better friend to those closest to me!

I have a very tight circle of my closest friends. *They are family.* These are the kinds of people I would do anything for, and I know they would do anything for me. Their kindness in intangible ways provides me with a judgment-free zone, the best hugs, and opportunities to cry or vent on the phone for an hour. These are the friends who let me crash in their spare rooms, anywhere from a night to moving in for several months, rent-free. They've surprised me with gifts, decorated the room I am staying in for my birthday, and written heartfelt cards I've kept for years. These were some of the first to invest in my dreams of one day moving to New York and being on national TV; they believed in me and strengthened me with confident love. They know just the right things to say. I love gifts and girl trips and priceless advice and conversation. It all makes me truly grateful.

KINDNESS ISN'T ABOUT CONVENIENCE.

If you want friends like this start *being* a friend like this! Just start doing more for your close friends and architecting the kinds of relationships you want in your life. Most of us will vision board our career or dream home, but we need to vision board our relationships too. That kind of intention has led me to make time.

A lot of times I'm in cities where people I know and love live, but I barely have the time to connect with them. I'll call and ask if they are willing to give me a ride to or from the airport or to the assigned location for work, instead of me getting a car service. It's a chance for me and my friends to connect. While they are giving to me, I'm able to give them the gift of time.

One of the girls I mentor was living in LA and I had a shoot.

I flew in that morning and had just enough time to get to her, drive to a Starbucks, order a couple of drinks, and give her a hug. It was doubly important because she'd had a death in the family and was feeling down. Kindness isn't about convenience. It's about thoughtfulness and quality fit into the time available. You can change someone's day, their perspective, and their mind in a minute.

Other moments in life require much more of a time commitment. One of my close friends, Samantha, and her husband were traveling to South Africa for his fortieth birthday. It would be a once-in-a-lifetime kind of adventure. They were excited about the safaris and tours they would enjoy. They would need to get a nanny for all five of their kids.

"Who is watching your kids?" I asked.

"Oh, I don't know yet, we'll figure it out," Samantha replied.

"Well, if you want, I wouldn't mind watching them for part of the time. Two weeks is a long time for one babysitter watching five kids."

She looked at me as if I was half-joking. I sent an email to my job asking for some time off, then I reminded her it was done, and I would be there for seven days to babysit their brood while they were away. Frankly, I barely gave it a second thought. As much as I enjoy children, I hadn't babysat in years, and I certainly wasn't thinking of five children, let alone their massive chocolate Labrador. It began to seem a bit extreme as the date moved closer: I was being asked to travel to Prague for an interview and would fly back just in time to take the nanny baton from the other sitter. Five kids whose homework I would have to check, drive to soccer games, and make dinner for—plus do the laundry, comb their hair, and take care of the dog!

The first day felt like a slumber party. We went to Disney on Ice, then to Starbucks, and then to soccer practice for one child while the rest of us enjoyed ice cream on a picnic blanket. Then we went shopping and I got dinner at a drive-in. Fun stuff.

On day two, things got real when I "lost" one of them. Somehow, no one saw the five-year-old get out of the car. I went back to the van. He wasn't there. Turns out he can run pretty fast. No biggie. I caught up to him and all was well. Later that afternoon, we went to the grocery store to buy sandwiches and fruit to have a picnic at the park. They had never had a picnic lunch and were excited.

"Miss Adrienne, I need to use the bathroom."

I was sitting down with my purse and keys and all the food and four other children I had to keep an eye on. Also, I had already sent two of them to the bathroom.

"Allie, please go with your sister to the bathroom, since you know where it is."

All was calm until I saw just one child, walking alone. "Where is your sister?" I asked.

"I don't know. She just left and went the other way when I told her to come this way."

Yes, I freaked out this time. Sister number one deciding to leave sister number two after using a public restroom was about the worst thing that I could hear. I went back with sister number one and asked the older ones to watch the others. Now, I did find sister number two wandering on the other side of the park trying to get to us without *any* worry or concern. I lost my cool a few times and realized I didn't want to raise five children all at once! (It had been a dream at one time.) By the end I had many of the emotions parents do: wondering if I'd done a good enough job, experiencing feelings of separation anxiety after coming back home to New York, and feeling absolutely no guilt about leaving ten loads of unfolded laundry. (I was just grateful I had managed to get it washed!)

It wasn't all stressful. I surprised them with an impromptu visit to the pond, threw a quick birthday party in the living room with photo booth props and sparkling cider (every kid thinks this is so fancy), and had the sweetest, most touching conversations with each one of them. Getting to know these smart, energetic, passionate, unique humans made me love them more. I baked a cake with the eldest and helped the second youngest make homemade slime. It was fun, chaotic, wonderful, and educational. Kindness blinded me to how hard it would be and gave me the stamina to wake up with that little tribe every day. Though I was exhausted, I was empowered too.

What a privilege to get a real gut check of what working moms go through in balancing housework, raising kids, and helping with homework! It was like going to parenting boot camp. We encourage young people to job shadow in order to determine whether they want to work in a specific industry. This would be a great way to help those longing to have children become more prepared for the responsibility. It helped give me a vision for motherhood and more compassion for women. I couldn't go on autopilot; I had to be alert. I have worked in high-pressure environments my whole career, and this was an experience of pressure that no one can explain to you. Some things you just have to *do*. It was like going to the gym and working different muscle groups and realizing where I wasn't in shape. It was a priceless opportunity.

Friends Are Investors

Being a friend to all creates a capacity to receive greater levels of friendship. As we develop, we realize how important it is that a relationship is not one-sided.

My friend Kristen, one of the women who invested the most in me at what I would call the most developmental point of my career, was always giving me advice and keeping me calm when I didn't know how I would get from point A to point B. Kristen was both a friend and mentor to me. She gave me personal advice about how to have more confidence and establish a more secure sense of identity. She taught me how to be a better communicator. She was also there to help me get my game face on when I was challenged with something at work. While you are pursuing a dream, you need those people in your corner who will tell you you're winning when you feel like you're losing, especially when it seems like the dream is drifting farther and farther away. There were other times we were just two girls who wanted to have some good Thai food—that was Kristen. Because we had such different personalities but common interests (mainly people and pad Thai!), we bonded. We ended up doing a lot of volunteering together. Because of her investment in me, I'm willing to do anything for her.

One golden lesson she taught me is: Know your players. It was usually brought up when we would have a meeting with volunteers or community members or at work when someone would come off as being less than open to ideas or would try to take over when the team seemed passive. What was bottled up in that one sentence was that we should be aware of each other, of our strengths and weaknesses and various personalities.

Many times, I have witnessed people just pushing through the personality part of the equation. No matter what happened in the meeting, there was someone with the authority to make a decision whether everyone was on board or not. The job would still get done, but it was usually evident that we did not have a heart for working together. We all knew who liked each other and who couldn't stand each other.

What Kristen taught me was how to flow with different kinds of people, and how to defuse a situation or react in a mature way. Believe me, it takes practice, and I continue to need more practice! But one key way of investing in people is allowing them to think differently than us and for it to be OK. One friend or colleague might always begin to tune out about fifteen minutes into any meeting. That's the person you want to give the floor to or allow to speak first before they get burned out. Another colleague might have great ideas and likes to take the credit for them but has no social graces. It's best to have them email their ideas to you before the meeting, then mention them by name to give the kudos needed without letting them get on their soapbox in front of people they may alienate themselves further from. There could be the one who is the comic, who is well liked and always the life of the party but gets easily distracted during business calls, which starts to turn the meeting. They may be perfect as the one who can initiate the icebreaker or speak at the end of the meeting as a way to present celebratory announcements and end the meeting on a high, fun note. We all have strengths and weaknesses. Rather than judge each other, we need to be kind and be a friend who allows imperfect people to be a part of the team without writing them off.

We should know the motivations of our colleagues, associates, and dearest friends—and also know what makes them tick. Instead of just anticipating that they will show up with a particular attitude or approach to things, we should be tuned-in enough to know what they like and dislike and when they are having a good or bad day. Because of the lesson of "know your players," I know Kristen and understand that what she occasionally needs is a creative outlet. When she is overworked, she needs to step back and do something arts and crafts related. It helps keep her cheery and people-focused rather than task-oriented.

One day, Kristen was talking to me about all the business she was doing. Somehow, she had managed to craft a couple of wreaths for the holiday and posted them online.

"Kristen, those are amazing! You know, if you build them up a little more, you could sell them," I said.

"You think so?" she asked. "I really just love doing them. You know me, I just need to *make* something here and there."

"Listen, I will Venmo you some money tonight. I'll be your first investor," I said.

Not only did she go straight to the crafts store and buy enough to make several wreaths, she felt so recharged she was able to accomplish more at work.

Two days later, Kristen called me.

"Suzie and Todd have been too busy to put up Christmas lights. I think with all they do for us, it would be really great if a bunch of us paid for their lights and put them up."

Kristen had noticed that time was running out for the family to enjoy the holiday decorations their kids were so excited to see, and that this act of kindness would be a way to show appreciation in a way that involved a whole community of people. So many friends came together that we had money to put in their greeting card, and the whole family enjoyed the display. What's important to mention is that there were cycles of investments here. Kristen invested in me for years, and I loved being able to invest in her wreaths. Suzie and Todd had let me live with them before, when I was in between cities and jobs, so contributing to the Christmas lights was easy to say yes to.

Investors hang around other investors. There was a time when one of my friends, Kayla, called me to ask if I would recommend a hairstylist for another woman who had a similar hair texture as mine. Toya was a single mom and getting her hair done was the last priority on her mind. Kayla asked if I was willing to chip in, along with several other women, to pay for an expensive treatment for Toya's hair. It was more than a gift. It gave Toya vision to take better care of herself, and she's been getting her hair done every month since. This and other kindnesses have led to her self-esteem skyrocketing. She has the best paying job she has ever had and can afford private school tuition for her daughter. It all started with a friend who knew she needed a nudge to see that *investing in herself* was worth it.

Here are some ideas for studying and investing in the people you spend time with:

Learn how they like their coffee. One of my managers enjoys a tall black coffee with milk. I am not always around them, but I know based on the amount of work they have, it's almost always a pleasant surprise first thing in the morning. One of my friends has been doing different diets over the years, so it's more complicated to get her coffee order. She's still worth getting a venti for!

Give gifts to people. Even if you don't know what they like, there's something about giving that allows for a new perspective. If possible, take time to ask someone who knows them best about their favorite things. A card and a candle are usually well-received. I once was out with the producer of a long-standing journalist. We talked about the journalist's likes, and she said, "He gives great gifts. But I just feel like he has everything, and I don't know that anything I could give would be nice enough." That producer ended up making a donation to the journalist's favorite charity as a gift in his name.

Have a chat with someone whose personality is completely different than yours. There are people who can simply rub you the wrong way, or you might just see a weakness in them and feel you're not the one to help them. A classmate, coworker, or neighbor who doesn't even know they need help can seem like work. But we all are needy for something. Compassion leads to understanding.

Treat your friend's interests and pursuits like your own. One of my friend's sons had a goal of giving $1,000 toward a school fundraiser. That's a lot of extra money for even some adults to fathom. I knew that any amount I gave would be an encouragement to him and to his parents as he grew in giving to others.

Friends and Likes

Most of us have a love-hate relationship with social media. We are grateful for the ease of sending a quick note or keeping family up to date on Instagram or Facebook, and we can get caught up with the day's news in a minute on Twitter. Then there are the minutes and hours we know we are wasting, scouring other people's feeds, playing games, and watching content for the sake of diversion from the day's work. There can also be negative, nasty comments from everyone, including trolls, bots, or your second cousin twice removed. Still, social media can be a vehicle for kindness.

Cynthia Smoot, a blogger and brand consultant in Dallas, Texas, and I were having a conversation around a bonfire with a few friends when she made an unexpected assessment. "You know, when social media first came out, it was for the purpose of connecting people. Then over several years we have seen stories and statistics about how we are more alienated by technology than ever before. Because of apps and platforms like Facebook, Twitter, Instagram, and Snapchat, industry experts say that people are more isolated and less relatable."

"Never mind the kinds of hateful, divisive things people post on those platforms," her husband, Randy, chimed in.

"But when you go around the room, most of the people who are here are people you initially connected with on social media, and then reached out to in the real world," Cynthia continued. "Adrienne, you're using social media for what it was intended for. The best use of social media. The other day I commented on your post and shared it, and you sent me a text message. I really appreciated that."

Going around that room, a couple of women were those I had met first on Twitter, one with a direct message because we had a mutual connection and she thought it would be great for networking. Somehow, after many months, or possibly years, we agreed to meet in a hotel lobby and discuss life, relationships, and letting go of the past. The tweeting stopped and I would instead send encouraging texts to check in or invite her to an online course I was attending.

SOCIAL MEDIA CAN BE A VEHICLE FOR KINDNESS.

Another was a college student who confessed she "slid into my DMs" and responded to a post I had shared asking people if they wanted coaching. I began to quietly mentor her. Another met me at a TV station event when I worked as a local news anchor in Dallas. We took a photo and then started messaging over Twitter. Years later she responded to an inspirational post I had shared, and I offered to mentor her. There were others who reached out to me via email and direct message and then we got to know each other IRL (in real life). I hadn't given it a thought until Cynthia made the case. You won't get to know every single person on your "friends" list like this, but being sensitive to when you can helps social media make sense. I've carried this kindness over when different people contact me.

We use apps now to meet new people to date and become friends with because it seems that real life for a lot of people has become more challenging in terms of finding your tribe. Here are some relationship tips that maximize the social media component:

Identify your tribe. Whether it's motivational speaking, fashion blogging, or gardening, find the groups that suit your interests. One of the tribes I ascribe to is beauty and skincare/aesthetics. I posted on my social media accounts that I would be at a spa, and one of the guests came up to me to thank me for sharing the event. I learned she'd been needing a new place to get a facial. I also learned she needed some direction in life. I shared resources for personal coaching, which led to a new career, a new outlook, and better friends.

Post only what you would not mind being broadcast on national television. See your conversations with this person on DM as synonymous with a public post. Sometimes social media can give us a sense of being unwatched or extra private, but since everything can be screen shot, treat it as public even if it is personal.

See your phone number and email as precious. Social media creates a way to get to know someone before giving out a ton of personal info. Don't feel obligated to give out your number first. Allow yourself to get to know the person first on private message.

Meet IRL in public. Coordinating time to meet that person face-to-face for the first several times should be in a public place, preferably with other people. You don't have to live in fear, but you do want to use wisdom.

Be aware if you see a post that causes concern and take the comments offline. As Cynthia mentioned to me, she was touched when I noticed a post and texted her directly. With our IRL friends who we know more about, we should be sensitive enough to know when they are posting something that is an unspoken prayer or cry for help. Rather than comment in the public section "Are you ok?" which can (A) be lost in the other messages, and (B) put a red flag out to others about something that is none of their business, send a DM, text, or email to check in, or call them personally.

It's important not to get too busy that we don't notice when someone is having a rough time. There are ways to be discreet and take a conversation offline to show you care beyond the thumbs-up emoji or liking a comment. Social media can be a starting point to helping someone in need. There is no better time to be a friend.

CHAPTER 9

KIND TO YOUR CREW: ALLIES AT WORK

Creating a kind environment at work initiates greater productivity and promotes happiness.

Many of us, if not all of us, fall prey to career baggage. We carry the negative words or memories that a previous coworker or manager has spoken to us in the past and are still scarred from it today! I have been in situations where people who work tirelessly are not respected. I have seen times when colleagues who were not shown the proper amount of appreciation on the job refuse to give their best today in a kind of twisted payback. Sometimes it is because of interactions with difficult people. We may have taken an offense when colleagues seemed to be cruel or bossy. While we cannot change the past, we can be empowered to work well in teams and to spark loyalty and unity. It's true for all of us—it's a lot more beneficial when you actually are interested in the project and even more beneficial to enjoy who you're working with! It makes the days go by much more smoothly. The following stories carry universal lessons and truths that will inspire you to kindness.

Remember Me

I was flown out to California from New York for a shoot with a producer and a three-man crew: Greg, Jeff, and Gary. I'd worked with Greg quite a bit while in Los Angeles. Jeff I'd worked with before as well but remembered by face only. I quickly introduced myself to Gary.

Always look people straight in the eye when you meet or when you are being reintroduced. One quick kindness rule of thumb: Do not start a conversation by asking, "What's your name again?" It is better to say, "I remember you."

Being remembered is important to everyone and it is a happier note to start on than asking a question that some might expect or hope you already know the answer to. Even if you do not remember their name, you show that you were not so busy as to forget that you *did* meet at one time, and that is what you want to focus on. It is one of the greatest compliments to acknowledge that someone was memorable.

Additionally, for any team to build a kind rapport, ask the crew for their input. Trust is built by asking the members of your team what they think even if they don't have the final word on the matter. Do not do it to placate them. It is kind to ask for and then listen to another person's perspective. I ask my photographers what they think of certain shots. I'm big on getting their feedback, because if it's not going to work, they should feel comfortable saying so. On this shoot, I asked the crew their opinion about me speaking while on a tree swing. (I wish I could show you a photo; it was awesome.) I didn't want it to be cheesy, but I was having so much fun on this swing on camera. The whole team thought it was great, and we ended up using a clip of me being a big kid in the story on air. (Everyone needs a swing in their yard!)

At the end of a day of shooting, we were waiting for the crowd to gather at a block party held in a nearby park. The group we had interviewed encouraged us to make ourselves at home and have some food. Without question, it was time for a break.

"You guys put all your stuff down and go grab a bite to eat. I'll watch the gear," I told them.

I think these three big guys barely ate, but I could tell it was the thought that they appreciated. The best teams are those who mix talent with a good time. We sat down and took a break for a few minutes. One of them gave me a big compliment about another project I was working on. Once we were done, I thanked them all with handshakes and hugs.

THE THOUGHT CAME TO ME: *IF HE WAS MY BROTHER, I WOULD HELP HIM OUT.*

While walking from the shoot location that day, I passed by one of the vendors. He stopped to ask me if I knew where the nearest bathroom was, just as I was leaving to grab my luggage and head to the airport. "Give me one minute; I'll ask," I said.

To be honest, I didn't think I was the best person to ask. Someone local at the park would have been more likely to know. Then the thought came to me: *If he was my brother, I would help him out*. So I went back into the park and first asked the women I had just interviewed if there was a public restroom nearby. (That answer was no.) I asked if it would be OK to go back to one of the couple's homes; I knew one of the women's husbands was still inside, and it felt safer to go back with him there. She agreed. As we walked through the park, I learned this vendor, Michael, was leaving the next week to be a paratrooper in the US Army. I shared stories about friends who had served and gave him some advice on leadership. As I grabbed my bag to leave, he gave me a hug and thanked me for helping him and for the words. When you are more supportive of those you work closest with, you'll automatically become supportive of others around you as well.

The Backstory

Years prior, at my first and only internship, I worked with Sam, one of the most experienced and hardened news photographers in Los Angeles. He was tough, icy, and he could be almost degrading—but I learned a lot from him. Including this: "Always take care of your crew and they'll take care of you." He told me to always remember to feed the crew—bring in a pizza or donuts—and to thank them. Show appreciation and you'll receive appreciation. Whatever you are looking for from your team, give it to them in turn.

ALWAYS TAKE CARE OF YOUR CREW AND THEY'LL TAKE CARE OF YOU.
—Sam

It didn't feel like it at the time, but Sam's seemingly unkind style was one of the best things to happen in my career. People raising their voices or getting upset on the job no longer caused me to panic. I definitely had thicker skin. And Sam's message of being kind and taking care of the crew was knowledge I needed to nurture. I occasionally forgot the lesson; for example, when I complained about the attitude of some of our more seasoned photographers. They grumbled, then I grumbled. That was a mistake. No matter what business you are in, it doesn't help to join in on the negativity. Sometimes we are the cause of that negativity ourselves and fail to grasp how our attitude is hurting other people.

It all stuck with me. Years later, I was working in TV and my mentor advised me to ghostwrite columns in the community paper he ran. I also volunteered to shoot video for nonprofits and community events. He told me, "I'm going to have you edit, shoot, and write better than anyone else I know. I want you to know exactly what your crew is going through so that you can empathize with them."

Refusing to Give In to Haters

That would pay off years later when I had some of the most tumultuous crew experiences of my life. Upon arriving at one station, I had a former colleague call me up to tell me there were rumors swirling about me: certain people, including a particular photographer, didn't like me, and were already saying some pretty harsh words to other coworkers. Another friend called to say there were some who thought I was trying to take someone else's job. None of it was true.

I had to learn to be tough enough to not flinch. Kindness gives us the power to override feelings, but the pressure I went through because of this was a major distraction. When you let what others say and do affect you, that is when you start to be depleted. This time of my career taught me to be conscious at work, that every move means something—even the most seemingly private and innocuous conversation in a news van with one other person. While recently talking to a crew, we discussed how you never know if someone is going to take what you say and use it against you on the job, even if you didn't have any wrong intentions. "There is no safe place," they all said.

THE ONLY SAFE PLACE ANYWHERE TODAY IS THE PLACE OF KINDNESS.

I was reminded that the only *safe place anywhere today is the place of kindness.* If it is not kind, I simply cannot afford it. When I am kind, even if someone tries—my words cannot be manipulated, weaponized, or compromised. It's not because I am walking on eggshells or trying to impress people; it is because I am being exactly who I am, and I know that what I say and do every day matters. I endeavor to live my life as if everything I say can be recorded or reprinted. I laid out a code of conduct for myself that you can duplicate in your team:

Code of Conduct #1: Never say an unkind thing about anyone, ever. If someone starts gossiping to you, you don't have to say, "I do not gossip." Just look away, look to your notes, get on your phone, or look at them and shake your head, but do not respond verbally. You can try to change the subject. I apply this even with my friends. Gossip can be far too easy to enter into and is destructive to company culture. It is something that most everyone has done in their life, usually as a result of being exposed to it. The people who gossip are not bad people; sometimes they think they are doing you a favor. Never say an unkind thing about your work partner, even if it is true. Treat them with dignity, even if you see an area they can grow in.

Code of Conduct #2: Treat older staff with the utmost respect. For me, older staff included my more experienced photographers, some of whom had covered foreign wars and the Watts Riots and had been in the business longer than I have been alive. I treated them all like professors before I treated them like peers because they know things it would take me years to know. I listened and took notes. I avoided calling them *sir* or *ma'am*. Most of them hated that, especially coming from a young woman who looked like she could be their daughter. Instead, I honored the fact that older colleagues have been around the block, offered to buy coffee every now and then, and showed a genuine interest in their lives. Checking on them and paying attention to what they said about family or work went a long way.

Code of Conduct #3: Decide that inside every grouchy person is a lovely human. Typically, management will send someone "green" out with the most experienced staffer, the one most known for their no-nonsense demeanor or toughness. Often these are the most passionate people in our business. They are the best, and because of their experience (having seen the best and the absolute worst in humanity), they are possibly the most jaded. After coming in very young and gifted, they have many times been chewed up and spit out over life's journey. They are also often the most innovative and visionary. However, because of time and trials, they've picked up habits some consider lazy. If it seems they are on constant smoke or meal breaks, it could be because they are so talented and experienced, they can do what it takes to get the job done in their sleep. They might appear to move a lot slower, but they are often mentally faster than their younger colleagues because of years of experience and repetition. They can be more difficult to manage because they are nearly indispensable, yet they don't always get along with others.

People skills are not formulaic, but these skills are some of the most vital. Some in the business world determine that those who are difficult to work with are a lost cause. But I have found that respect goes a long way in bringing out the best in people; it displays a belief that someone is worth the effort. Simply believe in everyone, instead of mentally giving up on them. Even if the difficult one is adamantly against everything you stand for, you can be the difference maker who quietly and confidently whispers—in spite of being yelled at, left hanging, or betrayed—"You will learn to love me."

I have now worked with every kind of personality and have learned from the sweethearts and the stubborn. (Besides, we *all* have our quirks, right?) I have chosen to get stronger and more seasoned with every crew I work with. It's about giving them dignity. It works every time. That consideration will spill over to helping anyone around you.

Kindness Is Not Magic or Manipulative

The result of people knowing that you have their back will result in them almost always having yours. There are exceptions, though. There are people who will still be a challenge to work with, no matter how kind you are. They may be ignorant of how they truly make things difficult, or they may be blatantly against you. Either way, you must refuse to change who *you* really are. Your kindness must remain intact. Someone told me a story about a person they worked with. Most considered this person nice, but in the right scenario and after a certain amount of time, they would become impatient and lose their temper and become mean. They described how this same person was able to flip from fuming mad to the kind of voice you might hear from a golf announcer. They would say that everything was fine—especially when communicating to managers—but in the field they would say and do things that were thoughtless and coldhearted. Kindness does not make the world perfect. However, kindness will protect you from becoming jaded and heartless. What someone says can be hurtful; they might even lie about you. But if you follow this code of conduct, you won't lose *yourself*. Kindness makes you unshakeable.

KINDNESS WILL PROTECT YOU FROM BECOMING JADED AND HEARTLESS.

Soft Skills

One weekday at *Good Morning America*, my social media producer and I were getting ready to do a Facebook Live interview. The moment we walked in for our live segment online, our usually gregarious photography intern, who should have been in the studio taking photos, appeared uncharacteristically melancholy. When I greeted her, she didn't reciprocate. No one in the room seemed to notice, though I did. However, I was off to report on live television and then had to leave. I thought about whether I needed to ask what was wrong. Some people are simply closed off and would prefer people not get in their business.

When I was finished with my story, there she was again. I noticed that she was still looking down. I looked at her intently and asked what was wrong. This time I could see how fragile she was. It looked as if someone had died. She quietly admitted her concern: "It's that I know I'm leaving New York. I have a visa for this internship but without full-time work I have to go back.

I tried to get an extension, but I'll be leaving in June. I want to stay. There are no jobs in my country; not doing this."

I motioned for her to follow me into a room where she could have privacy. I didn't give her much of a choice. We talked. I encouraged her and gave her a huge hug. I looked at her and was prompted to ask about the jewelry she was wearing, partly to get her to talk about something that would make her smile. Around her neck were several gold necklaces with pendants. "Who gave you these?" I asked.

"These? They are from my grandmother."

"Well, if she were here, she would call you by her favorite nickname for you. She would hug you and tell you that, somehow, everything is going to be OK, wouldn't she?"

She nodded. I passed her a tissue as she cried.

"Oh my goodness, Adrienne, thank you. I needed that. Now I have got to pull myself together!"

"I couldn't help but notice you were going through something," I said.

"Thank you for your help. I didn't know what to do. Thank you so much."

People are surprised by a gentle touch and usually even more surprised that someone will take time out of their busy life to check on them. Speak encouragement to someone and believe that spontaneous, big, good things can and will happen. There are times we need more than the right job, the right connections, and the right friends. We need someone to notice us.

The day wasn't over yet. I left the studios, took a nap, and made it back into the office. One of my appointments was meeting my former intern from the first news job I ever had; she was visiting family on the East Coast.

She asked what I was up to and I told her the story of the intern from just that morning; I knew she could relate. It had been seven years and she was finally getting a full-time media job in Los Angeles.

The weight of that hit me. I have learned to take deep breaths when I need to take a pause, even if for a second. I counted: *one, one thousand.*

I had received my first on-air job—a once-a-month TV host position in Los Angeles—just a couple months out of school at the University of Southern California, then my first full-time staff position two years later in my hometown, which just happened to be the twentieth largest television market in the country. Now I was on a national network, doing what I always dreamed I would do. My grandparents and all my family could watch me on TV and see all the hard work had paid off. I took another deep breath.

Two, one thousand.

"What is it like? I mean, being at this level?" she asked.

On this day I realized that very seldom did I celebrate. I still saw so much to climb for. In that moment I saw how far I had come, and it was amazing! It was also agonizing.

"It's wonderful," I told her, "and it's tough. It's as though you're on another planet and you're tested every day. It's the hardest thing I've ever done."

I took a deep breath again. As the sunlight danced around us outside that coffee shop, I let the buildings on the Upper West Side of Manhattan come into focus. I remembered being in Sacramento, California, where I met this student—now a woman with a job in media, still looking up to me for advice all these years later. I had seen many people in our business try to talk young people out of getting into TV and journalism. I realized sitting there that part of the reason she was looking to me is because I had been kind to her, using a gentle approach. She wasn't looking for me to sugarcoat it, but the kind thing for me to do was tell her it was all worth it in the long run, that working in this business had its rewards, and to give her some sense that she was going to be okay. It was a full-circle moment and I was taking it all in.

Three, one thousand.

"Let me give you some good advice, even though you haven't asked for it."

She smiled with her eyes as she usually did when she braced herself for something important.

"Be softer," I said. "I know you're fierce and independent and tough, and you emulate that. You look like you're equipped to come to the rescue and do anything you're asked."

She smiled, again.

"A lot of people in this business are hard. They are all those things you are; they are ready for anything—only many of them are hurting. They've given up everything to be 'here' and it isn't quite what they hoped for. They've wanted love, and it didn't work out. They wanted kids, and it didn't work out. They wanted a title, a position, a voice. Maybe they never got those things. Some of them did; and even with all the amazing experiences and the great doors that have opened for them, they are still not quite fulfilled. However, they are really good at their jobs."

I WANT YOU TO NOTICE PEOPLE, NO MATTER HOW BUSY OR HOW HARD THE BUSINESS IS.

I paused. "I want you to be soft. I want you to be kind. I want you to notice people, no matter how busy or how hard the business is. What this hard business needs is kind people. People who do not get too busy or stressed to take the time to ask what's wrong. You know why?"

"Why?"

"Because the world is looking for people who are kind enough to stop, be aware, and take notice. They are looking for an ally and for hope. With all of the spectacular things we do and see in this world, sometimes the most shocking and electrifying thing we see is the surprise of someone who truly engages and connects with us in a generous way without asking for anything in return."

She nodded in agreement. However, in a blink of an eye, my former intern brought something to my attention that day without even realizing it. While taking the time to stop and be empathetic, we need to be empathetic with ourselves. I needed to take a second (or ten) to breathe, and to remember that even though life is work, it is a joy as well. Reflecting on the fact that she had been with me while a college student, seeing her growth reminded me of what I was like at the start of my career. We can lose some of the fun and inquisitiveness over the course of a challenging journey, and yet it only takes a second to flash back and remember how excited we were to move to a big city and pursue what looked like an impossible dream. Take a moment and remember to soak it all in with gratitude and to rehearse your wins. This will help you to be more at peace with yourself and work better with others.

Kindness Comes to Help Us

There are going to be plenty of days when your peace is challenged.

It was a busy weekday at the *Good Morning America* studios. I had just walked offstage. No matter what I am feeling, I am focused on showing up for the audience in the studio and at home, and I give it my all. I looked into the camera and read that script off the teleprompter like someone watching depended on it. When you are on the air, there are levels of excitement and stress that build, and then it's over in a matter of seconds or minutes. There are so many stagehands and audio engineers, grips and cameramen who follow our every move, replace the chairs and sofas on stage, adjust microphones on our lapel, hand us a water or hot coffee, and high five us on the way to delivering the news. Our *Good Morning America* stage directors, Eddie, Fonzie, and Brad, tell us where to stand and which camera to turn to, and they are keenly aware of whether people are in position or not.

On this particular morning, Fonzie asked, "How was your story?"

I was surprised by the question. I didn't expect anyone to ask how my time on television went, since once you were done, there were more stories to get on the air and people were intensely busy. The flurry of activity would blow by you like a hurricane. I was also taken aback because it was a day that I was less than impressed with my own delivery. One thing that we all can be is too harsh a critic of ourselves. Instead of complaining or being down on myself, his question snapped me back to reality. It was kind of him to ask. His question helped me to stop overanalyzing and remember the big picture.

"How could it have gone anything but fabulous with a great crew like you all?" I said.

He started shaking his head with a perplexed look on his face. "Oh no," he said emphatically. "You don't need us; you do a great job all by yourself."

I didn't miss a beat. "Fonzie, don't you ever for a second think that we who are on camera do anything on our own. When people behind the scenes are thoughtful and say good morning to us, when you are calm and kind when we have only minutes to get to the set, when you are patient with us and tell us we look nice, all of that contributes to an atmosphere that is more conducive to us getting out there and making some TV magic. You create the environment so I can do my job better, Fonz!"

I have made it my mantra and shared it with many of my fellow employees: "There are no insignificant jobs in television." Everyone in any profession holds a significant position, from the janitor to the president. Fonzie smiled as he turned to walk quickly down the hall. The show wasn't over yet.

"You're the best, AB," he said. "Have a great day."

Reflecting on it, I can't prove he needed encouragement, but I wouldn't be surprised if that was the case. What I do know is the less than two-minute conversation in the hall helped both of us.

Wherever you work, every person has the power to make a huge difference, if only for the fact that every person's temperament affects the rest of the team. One optimistic person can become contagious. One stressed-out person is able to spread negativity. Just as it's a producer's job to prepare us with what we need to go on camera, I have made it my position to stay focused and calm so that when I come to work, I deliver kindness and peace and remain tuned in to what people are feeling and going through so I can respond thoughtfully and correctly.

THE LESS THAN TWO-MINUTE CONVERSATION IN THE HALL HELPED BOTH OF US.

I will never forget the story of one of my engineers from one of my first news stations. Jim was almost always sweet and funny when he came into work. One day I walked by him in the hall, and he was angry and snapped at me. I was fuming inside and thinking of what I could say. Instead I chose to keep my mouth shut and walked away. I learned later that his mother had died the night before. It is true that *you never know what people are going through*. It taught me not to take mistreatment personally. Kindness will make you more understanding of others and gentler everywhere, every day.

There was a time I was going through some personal struggles, and I was sleepy and came into work knowing I could be cranky if I wasn't careful. I told those immediately around me that I was not feeling my best. Even when you want to stay positive, it is a great practice to let people know you're working through some things, that you are in a battle or had a rough night, so that they know you are human! I have found it helps to receive help and initiate closeness. As soon as I mentioned how I was feeling, immediately one of my coworkers responded, "You need some water; you're probably dehydrated." She then made small talk with me over a ring I was wearing and told me of a wish she had for a specific piece of jewelry. It was nice to have a simple, open conversation with her. I realized the connection point was my openness to admit I wasn't feeling well, and her openness to be of help. She is a firstborn, and firstborns, especially big sisters, tend to respond well to situations where they can assist or help people.

There was another time when I just relaxed and chatted about how I knew I needed to take better care of my body and health. Seeing that we had something in common helped her relate to me. When people already see you as strong, extraordinary, and highly capable, it is a kindness to show them you have to fight to sleep the right amount of hours, force yourself to take your vitamins, and struggle to get out of bed and into the office!

I say this to all of my power players, especially the strong women who sometimes feel pressure to present an image that everything is fine. I do not suggest sharing all your personal business, especially at the office. However, there is simply a need for balance between sharing and displaying who we really are. It is extreme to never mention one thing about your life that could be improved or changed.

You will be doing yourself a favor by studying people. I've been researching birth order since I was about ten years old. It fascinated me that of my six siblings, all our personalities were so different. All of us were motivated by different things to convince us to do the dishes or set the table for dinner. It will pay for you to study what brings out the helper in your boss or coworkers. Are they more helpful when you go in with options for how to tackle a problem? Or are they more helpful when you ask questions? One group of people is more helpful when you make them feel like an expert, even when you are the more educated or experienced. Study those you work with. Bringing out the helper in them with your kindness and openness will make them more productive and easier to work with. I believe nearly everyone has a sense of initiative and compassion; they are just triggered by different things.

STUDY WHAT BRINGS OUT THE HELPER IN YOUR BOSS OR COWORKERS.

Have you ever seen a kind person who said they did not have the help they need? Sharing kindness has no adverse side effects, yet there are things we do inadvertently that overshadow the real magnetism that comes from kindness. People will be drawn to want to help you. You can cancel that out by doing what turns people in your family or on your team *off*. Remember, it is not people-pleasing, it is about coming to balance. I find high achievers tend to operate in extremes. If you want kindness to function at its peak, be balanced in your conversation, in making people feel comfortable, in your interests (sports, the arts, music), and in your ambition. Be *extreme* in kindness.

If you are kind but still not healed of insecurities, you'll get a reputation for being needy. If you are kind yet predominantly share only your victories, you're likely to be seen as boastful and self-serving. If you are kind yet have not completely done away with the habit of complaining, your negativity will eventually cause conflict. If you're always smiling without any real substance in your conversation, you might not be taken seriously. If you do not share enough of your story or invite people to get to know you, people may not trust you or buy into the undeniably kind person you are. In order to receive more help, be kind enough to see where these areas of your life could be balanced out, and you will find more people want to help you. *Balance comes by thinking long term and by giving.* You will find that your life is more in balance when you have a vision for the future. Here are a few examples:

- **BALANCE IN CONVERSATION:** Listen more than you talk. Avoid sharing your opinion and ask questions to increase learning.
- **BALANCE IN PASSION:** Our passions can become all-consuming, so make sure to allow time to listen to and invest in other people's passions and dreams in order to be a dream maker.
- **BALANCE IN INTEREST:** Whether sports, art, or food, schedule time for these interests while budgeting time for things that are longer-range pleasures, like increasing your stock portfolio.
- **BALANCE IN GOALS:** Take the time to work diligently on your personal development. To avoid being driven by selfish ambition, schedule time to volunteer and donate to charitable causes.

If you have a teachable heart, refuse to see anyone as unworthy, and treat everyone with respect rather than trying to be everyone's bestie. You won't always be invited out for the party, but you will win people over the long term. The key is being the real you, staying balanced, and not taking yourself or anything else too seriously.

Stories of Helpers

There is a movie I watch quite regularly in which Tori Spelling plays a TV host, and in one scene she says, "I want to thank some people. My wonderful, wonderful crew." Every once in a while, I can hear myself sounding exactly like Tori in my mind! A great team does make such a difference and cares so much.

One morning I went to the crew on *Weekend Good Morning America* and asked for a first aid kit. I was thinking they would point me in the right direction to find it. One of our crew, Charlie, seemed to jump up like he was struck by electricity. "They usually take everything out of this medicine cabinet; it'll be in the other one. You're going to be in hair and makeup, right? I'll go get it for you."

He was gone in a flash before I could answer any questions. In a matter of minutes, he was back; he'd run to at least two other first aid stations and brought me multiple little treatments that I needed—bandages, cooling pad, gauze, antibacterial ointment, and hydrocortisone cream. It was sweet that he was so thorough. A second stagehand came in and asked, "Do you need a water to take any pills?"

"Oh no. Thank you so much for asking," I replied. It was like I was the most important person in the world at that moment.

After the show, our photographer, who controls the cameras

remotely, stopped by the office I was in to say hello. "That top you're wearing is very nice. It looks so good on camera. The colors really pop," he said. "I made sure to widen your shot so you could see it all." He gestured with his hand.

It's these little moments of attention to detail from the crew that makes it so much better to come to work. I endeavor to acknowledge them, so they know I care and recognize their hard work.

Having Your Back

I often say that producers are the hardest-working people in the business. One morning I was assigned a last-minute story on the US Open. Within minutes I needed to know everything I could about the rules regarding a controversial tennis story. While live on TV later, one of the cohosts asked me a question about a different rule in tennis—and while I hadn't looked up those terms, I knew how to answer intelligently. No harm, no foul! Then came the next question from another cohost: "What was the score?"

I had not even looked that up. I was stumped! I answered: "I don't know the score—I was a little focused on this angle of the story!" The whole team had a laugh before I heard the director speaking in my ear, telling me to go to weather.

"Let's go to weather!" I exclaimed.

My cohosts and the entire crew were laughing. I was laughing too, but annoyed I had not researched the right answers in the mere minutes I had to get ready to go on air. I was determined, this would *not* happen to me again.

The next day I was assigned another US Open story. I was still waking up when I grabbed my phone and saw I had an email from one of the producers who wrote for many of the other anchors and correspondents. She often told me she loved when I sang on air and sometimes made requests after I belted out a line of Bruce Springsteen or Mariah Carey during an entertainment story. Once the entire audience sang along with me to a couple lines of Will Smith's *Fresh Prince of Bel Air* theme song, and she took the time to thank me personally. On this particular morning, she threw me a life preserver.

> 5:06 AM
>
> Good morning, my friend. As you know, you have a tag about the Williams sisters after your 7a piece. I don't know if you're a tennis fan, but I am a little bit and saw these nuggets.
>
> Serena and Venus face off Friday in the third round.
>
> It is their 16th time competing in a Grand Slam.
>
> They have now BROKEN the record for active rivalries.
>
> Venus is seeded 16, Serena is 17—neck and neck!

I was humbled and thankful she had my back. She was covering me and I knew it. Here's my response:

> 5:12 AM
>
> You are very kind. Thank you. With a little more time I was able to gather far more intel on the game. You doing this really means A LOT!!! You're the best! :)

Her next email was a simple one-liner.

> This is the thanks for singing.

CHAPTER 10

RESILIENCE IN A CRAZY WORLD

Kindness will keep you sane. The cure for anger, frustration, or disappointment is kindness.

"The world is crazy."

How many times have you heard someone say that in the past year? Everyone is under more and more pressure. Increasingly we are weighed down with the troubles of family members, the road rage of fellow commuters, and the violence we see everywhere. As I type, the second fatal synagogue shooting in six months has happened on US soil.

From highways to high-rises, people of every walk of life seem angrier and more out of control than ever. At work and home, people are losing their tempers, speaking in ways that are callous, discriminatory, or inflammatory. On social media and in the centers of previously peaceful towns, there have been full-scale culture wars, wars of ideology, and gunfights involving everything from police to arguments over a parking space. Every day, people are becoming more anxious and more emotionally unpredictable.

Unless we are *inoculated from anger*, any one of us is susceptible to losing our temper, decency, and common sense.

Kindness Is the Remedy

Kindness goes beyond pacifying us; it cures us of anger. When we are doing something kind for someone else, or thinking kind thoughts, or reflecting on a kindness someone has done for us, it keeps us from thinking about anything negative. That is why it is important to stay occupied with kind thoughts, and to have short-term memory loss for what upsets us.

While others are under stress and pressure that stirs anger, choose to be a peacemaker. You cannot change the way people act or feel. This is their decision. Your decision is kindness. It is a way of preventing an argument from happening or escalating. Several times in my career, people have been inconsiderate, which produces a real tension. Some people are blatantly disrespectful or say things that are completely inappropriate. Kindness can be quiet and at other times kindness can speak up. Many times, kindness expresses itself by a person acting as though they did not hear something said that could cause a debate or destruction to someone's character. I have seen it myself in others and I have needed to do it myself—when I simply acted oblivious to the situation or walked out of the room. Removing yourself from conversations that could cause you to join in on the negativity is kind to yourself and prevents you from entering a negative space.

UNLESS WE ARE INOCULATED FROM ANGER, ANY ONE OF US IS SUSCEPTIBLE TO LOSING OUR TEMPER, DECENCY, AND COMMON SENSE.

There are other times when you cannot remove yourself from a toxic environment. Too often I have seen people try to make other people feel better or attempt to stop conflict by agreeing or joining in on the negative talk. Instead of placating or enabling people, kindness will change the perspective with one statement or a question. When someone is upset, try saying something like this: "*We cannot control what other people do or how they treat us; I just know you are strong and resilient, and you've been able to get through tougher things than this.*"

By provoking them to a new thought on the matter and shifting the focus to compliment them rather than critique someone else, the words refresh rather than add fuel to the fire.

Feeling Out of Control

There are plenty of times when I myself have been angry that life was not going the way I wanted. Many of the choices we make are our own self-effort to try and do something that makes sense or to control our lives. The path to fulfillment is littered with hardship: We may not get the promotion or raise we think we deserve. We have a medical emergency that ends up depleting our savings. Factor in family, disappointments, and believing that you should be further along than you are now, and it can be a formula for a mental health emergency. Many of us are on the brink of "losing it" when we hit a wall and do not know how to stop feeling hopeless, depressed, or trapped in a dead end. The best thing to do when you are feeling frustrated is look for a kind expression. This is more than a random act of kindness. We need to plan kindness in our day just like we make the decision to brush our teeth—as a means to avoid a potential pity party and to realign with purpose.

Now first let me say it is great to be strong and confident when life looks almost as glittery as that video of you with a radiant Instagram filter—the one where you are all glowy, having a good hair day, and look like you're on top of the world. Your mentors love you, your colleagues respect you, and your kids are all dressed like baby models. However, your true strength will be revealed when you're facing the storms of life. When there are pressures and traumas pulling on you, it is easy to keep the focus on problems and on yourself. There will be days you won't want to get out of bed. We all have off days or days when we are not sure we are doing anything right. Our relationships can feel irreparably broken, our jobs can seem dead-end, or we are miserable, and we don't know why.

On my lousiest days, when I have felt like exhaustion or lack of motivation is hunting me down, it was kindness toward others that gave me *life*. Lousy can happen when you're in your dream job. In the midst of one of the high points in my career, my dad passed away the day before my birthday. A month before, my arm completely locked up in its socket and my hair started thinning and breaking off. I could explain it away because, after all, I was on television six days a week or more. It would make sense that my hair was being styled too often, and *that* is why my hair was breaking off. Maybe. The truth is, I was under an intense amount of stress. No one knew what I was going through at work. I traveled across the country to Los Angeles, then to

Toronto and London in a whirlwind of work trips. I was being told I was doing a great job, all while I battled bouts of guilt, regret, anger, and sorrow off camera.

Mental Wellness: Kindness Is Your Life Preserver

Two months before all this craziness happened, I had the amazing idea of investing in younger people who wanted to get insights for living their best life. I had partnered with four people in four different states to mentor them, starting right before I found out my dad was dying. We talked on a regular basis or communicated by email about their goals and strengths. At the same time, I had a regular mentoring group in New York that had reached the one-year mark. I was meeting weekly with a group of young, mostly media professionals who were looking to invest in themselves.

THE EMOTIONAL STORM I WAS IN CONTINUED TO RAGE; HOWEVER . . . KINDNESS TIED ME TO THE MAST OF MY SHIP AND PREVENTED ME FROM GOING OVERBOARD.

The consistency of giving to them kept me on a certain vibe of giving back, especially when my work schedule was so demanding and all over the place. Meanwhile, everything else in my personal life, including ambitions and vision, seemed to be hanging on by a thread. Even through all my battles, with kindness in focus, I always had a word to give my mentees. The advice I gave them was often an inspiration to me. I continued giving financially to nonprofits I believed in, even when I had less passion for the causes I was involved in, because I had a strong sense of commitment and would not let my emotions determine my actions. (I ended up giving my largest charitable gifts in this rocky year.) The emotional storm I was in continued to rage; however, generosity and consistent kindness tied me to the mast of my ship and prevented me from going overboard. I can't say that I had courage; these were some of the most tearful, crazy, chaotic moments I have ever lived. But being kind, even when I didn't feel like it, reiterated to me that my true identity, who I really am, would not let me down, even in moments where I had good reason to quit. It was in this time of testing that I decided I would be the kind of woman I wanted to be, in spite of intense evidence that I had every right to throw a tantrum, have an emotional breakdown, or let someone hear exactly what I thought about them. It was in this time I would be strengthened to be the woman I said I was, the best me, no matter what it looked like!

Perhaps you have had times like this in your life—when on the outside you were handling business and on the inside you were just holding it all together. When we are living on the edge, we need a superpower to keep us from slipping, because stress can deflate our confidence and upend our consistent routine. Because kindness is your wholehearted identity, it is an assured safety net. By shifting the focus to others, no matter how tough life gets, you'll catch a wave of hope that will breathe fresh oxygen and tenacity into you. Giving kindness is a reminder that you're not put on this earth to be miserable. You're put on this planet to shine bright and be

BY SHIFTING THE FOCUS TO OTHERS, NO MATTER HOW TOUGH LIFE GETS, YOU'LL CATCH A WAVE OF HOPE THAT WILL BREATHE FRESH OXYGEN AND TENACITY INTO YOU.

someone else's answer. When you provide the emergency raft to someone who is sinking, you are kept safe above the raging waters too. Kindness keeps you committed to being who you really are, at all costs, in spite of contrary feelings and down days. It's the superpower that keeps you connected to your true identity.

Kindness Brings Calm

I heard someone wise say, "Be a thermostat, not a thermometer." In essence we want to set the temperature in the room, not reflect the temperature. When emotions are running red-hot, a kind presence can be a cool breeze and change the way people feel and act. One huge benefit of kindness is that you have compassion and understanding, even while being wise about who you are dealing with. When you know your power, when you know that you cannot lose, cannot be harmed, and cannot be stopped, you bring a confidence and calm. You know that hurt people *hurt* people—and it is not personal.

Something my mentor helped me see is that no matter the environment, consider yourself ineligible for division. He encouraged me to initiate an attitude of "I'm with you." Stay on the side of peace. If people act in any way unkind to you, act as though you never noticed. Practice continuously looking for ways to bring more calm and more kindness, without a word.

One day at work I noticed a younger member of the team and she looked upset. She broke down crying after I pulled her into a conference room to talk. The pressure of deadlines and working seven days a week was wearing on her, and she felt one of the staff was being very difficult and mean. Another time a member of the team was visibly frustrated, angry over their career not going how they planned. They felt they were trapped, and it was causing them to feel they were on the edge of breaking down. Kindness gets ahead of the curve and helps bring reconciliation or peace to the one who is scared, hurting, angry, or hopeless. It helps them talk it out before they blow up in anger on the job and tarnish their whole career. When you notice someone displaying signs of edginess, stop and do more than ask how they are doing. Ask them directly, "Is there anything I can do for you?"

It will open them up to discuss what is bothering them. If you cannot do anything to help them, you can most certainly give them a hug, an encouraging word, or offer to buy them a coffee.

Kindness When Someone Dies

Death is like nothing else on the planet for either getting our attention or knocking us off our feet. It's interesting. I just stopped by the bank and a teller I've known for years whose father passed away months ago is still grieving. A longtime public relations friend I just happened to check in with told me of the death of a family member. When a loved one dies, it affects you in ways you don't quite see coming. It can hit like a freight train.

Death is something I did not truly experience until I was nineteen years old. I barely knew the people who died in my childhood and was only vaguely familiar with stories that sounded like movie plots. Two uncles out of the four brothers committed suicide; one died of a self-inflicted gunshot and drug use. Another jumped off a bridge to his death. Mental health, suicide, and those who have struggled with the loss of a loved one as a result of suicide are subjects that are still considered somewhat taboo. No matter how someone dies, those who survive the death need the comfort and mercy of community. I would only realize later that I struggled with death and was in denial of how hard it would be to cope once a parent or close loved one passed.

The first funeral I attended was that of a coworker. I was the last person he talked to before he died of a massive heart attack. He called in to the office within an hour of collapsing on his treadmill. Between this and the stories of my uncles, it was hard for me to face the funerals of those I loved. I didn't show up for my grandfather's funeral; it was too painful for me to think of losing him. For my two grandmothers, I found the courage to see them just in time. They both died within twenty-four hours of my visits.

All of this has given me a deep compassion for those who have dealt similarly with death. Know that you're not alone if you have struggled with paying your last respects. Please do whatever you need to do to overcome this fear or anxiety; ask a friend to go with you and express your concerns humbly. Tell them you are struggling with visiting the hospital or hospice.

I remember visiting a couple of colleagues' family members who only had days to live. That was easier for me. I believe it helped me to become more comfortable with seeing my loved ones for the last time. I always encourage people that if there is any way possible, make the time and the trip to say goodbye.

One of my dear friends was having a hard time planning a visit to see her mother while she was battling stage-three cancer. There was some hope that her mom would pull through, but it ended up being her final fight. Because of all my experiences with death in those last hours, I urged my friend to go sooner rather than later. I even bought her a plane ticket. Being kind to those who are grieving includes helping them override the paralyzing emotions of fear and regret.

Most people understandably have a very hard time with death and even more difficulty knowing what to say to those who are in mourning. Especially in a business setting, people are either prone to say absolutely nothing or send a card or email immediately following word of a memorial service. Then we all get busy. The only problem is, the effects of death on the bereaved's psyche can last months or longer. I've learned to check in with people after most have forgotten about their heartache.

KINDNESS TO SOMEONE WHEN THEY ARE GRIEVING MEANS LOOKING TO SEE HOW YOU CAN BRING A SENSE OF CONSISTENCY AND ROUTINE TO A TUMULTUOUS TIME.

These are the ways I have found to express kindness when someone dies:

I've found flowers are a huge lift to most people, but another thing I've done is buy a small book dealing with grief for those going through it. There are a number of books on the topic. It's a great way to express thoughtfulness and a practical way for a colleague or loved one to believe they are empowered with a tool to get through their time of mourning.

A phone call is much better than a text message at times like this, and the time to call is not typically upon hearing about the death. Schedule a time in your calendar to check up on them, perhaps a month following the funeral, then six to eight weeks later, and then another month or two after that. Set a reminder so that you don't forget to check in. Your intention will keep you focused on the needs of others.

Use airline miles and gift them to your friend or colleague.

It is highly likely that a person grieving is spending much more money on travel to see their family or help with the costs associated with burial, outstanding bills, or household matters. Start a conversation about what airline they most frequently use to visit family, or just give them a gift certificate. Your thoughtfulness will touch their heart in a major way and remove some of the financial burden. Do not think that because someone is in a high-paying job or position that they can afford to buy their own tickets. It is not about whether someone can pay for this or not; it is about coming alongside someone during a time they need help lifting that burden of grief.

Kindness to someone when they are grieving means looking to see how you can bring a sense of consistency and routine to a tumultuous time. Rather than taking them to lunch, consider a gift card for prepared meals or a service online that could deliver groceries so that they do not have to think of meals for themselves or their family. Grieving can put you in a state of shock, numbing you to the day-to-day responsibilities that would otherwise be simple. Think of the things that are every day and ask whether you can help. Here are some ideas in addition to meals:

1. Stop by their home and offer to take their car for a car wash or to fill the tank.
2. Offer to schedule a hair or nail salon appointment and personally take them to have a time of peace.
3. Offer to assist with daycare or childcare. You could accomplish this by paying for one day or one week; or by sending someone who has helped you in the past, like a trusted family member, to their home.
4. Offer to take them out for a run, spend time at the driving range, or take a spin or fitness class together as a way to decompress.

5. Offer to just come and sit with them. There is kindness in simply being with a person. There is the priceless gift of demonstrating to someone that they are not alone.
6. Give a friendly embrace. Put your arm around them and just smile. Even if you don't say a word, they will appreciate it.
7. Write a nice card and make it short and sweet. Words of affirmation are some people's love language. Sometimes, there is nothing better than a kind note that says, "I am here for you." You can also involve several people in your department or team and have each person write their own individual note.
8. Talk to people in your office about a possible fundraiser. For some, money is not an appropriate gift, but cash can be the best way to meet a need during a time of grief and unexpected expense. Ask everyone to give what is on their heart and you may be surprised at people's generosity.
9. Get creative about what you can do now to prepare for the passing of someone you care about. Some in your circle or family may consider it morbid, but planning for the inevitable will bring peace. If you do not have a will, no matter how young you are, consider what you would like done in your honor and what kind of service you would like. Ask your family what they would like done in terms of a memorial service and what the widow or widower would want to do that day. Would they like to go out to eat following the funeral or wake? Would they like to go to a movie or go for a road trip? Planning out how you will handle the death as a family on the day of a loved one's passing will provide some constancy to those who are closest to the deceased.

10. Remember to contact them during major holidays. A dear friend of mine lost her mother very close to Mother's Day. I called just to see if there was anything I could do to help make it a positive memory. She let me know she had plans, but this is a time when the simple act of calling will remind them that someone cares.

CHAPTER 11

RIGHT PLACE, RIGHT TIME

You know that familiar voice you hear when your navigation says, "Rerouting"? Kindness helps us reroute, especially in chaos.

Kindness is like GPS: it will lead and direct you, your schedule, and your day in a way that "going through the motions" never could. It also gives you a sixth sense, the results of which will almost make you look like a mind reader. The truth is, putting someone else first makes you keenly sensitive to the heartbeat and heart's desires of those you decide to partner with in kindness.

Spontaneous Selflessness

The first way this can manifest is by following warm impulses or spontaneous selflessness. An inclination to be kind can seem to come out of nowhere. I have a fond winter memory of deciding to make my way to a friend's studio to drop off a holiday card. I made a quick run to the pharmacy nearby to buy her a gift—something small like chocolate or a candle. Or maybe she would appreciate some lavender-scented soap. I thought, *Surely I will know it when I see it.* The only problem was, everything in those aisles seemed impersonal. I did not see anything that resembled what I would have bought for her. I started to walk out of the store, hoping the card was enough, when it occurred to me to buy her mascara.

That is weird even as I type it. Mascara? Makeup almost seemed too personal. After all, many people only like certain brands or only shop at department stores for their cosmetics. I was at the pharmacy checkout line and still debating if buying mascara would be appropriate or if I was just getting desperate to buy anything. I have never purchased mascara for anyone in my life. The next thought came to me: she could use the mascara as a kind of backup at her office in case she wasn't carrying her makeup bag . . . or needed to freshen up her look . . . or ran out of the house before finishing her makeup at home. With these thoughts I started making a case for what I would do next, because I could not shake the thought of buying her mascara! *Surely it cannot hurt to be wrong about getting someone mascara*, I told myself. If it is weird to her, it is still thoughtful. So I scanned the racks of makeup and found a tube that looked like she would wear it. I arrived at her office and handed her the card and the mascara and started to explain. I did not even need to.

"Just this morning I was thinking I should have some mascara at my office," she said. "When it's cold, my eyes tear up, and by the time I walk from the train station to my front door, all my mascara has come off! This is perfect, and I do not know how you knew."

When you act on warm impulses like this, some are going to be extremely impressed. Other times the recipient of your kindness is just going to say, "Thanks!" Either way, the point is this: by giving in to those warm impulses, you will position yourself in different places to deliver exactly the gift, encouragement, or word someone needs that day.

Another time a friend of mine in California had just had a baby. She was a little overwhelmed. This was baby number two; things were a little messy around the house. I remember getting off the phone feeling a deep empathy for how much my friend's life was changing, wondering what I could do to help thousands of miles away. I decided to call someone I knew who did some personal grocery shopping with a penchant for finding good deals. I asked if she would fill a couple bags with baby wipes, snacks, diapers—things a mom would need—when the thought randomly occurred to me to have her buy some ladies' razors too. I would hand-deliver these items to my friend the next time I was in her town.

This momma was so appreciative for the bags of baby stuff, but she screamed when she saw the razors. "Oh my goodness, Adrienne, how did you know I needed razors?" she shouted excitedly.

"I am telling you, I wanted to get you all baby stuff that would help with the newborn when this picture of disposable razors popped into my head," I told her.

"I haven't shaved my legs in I don't know how long!" she said. "I have had no time to go to the store. This is perfect!"

This was a great lesson for me to think of what a *mom* would need, not just what a new baby would need, because if momma ain't happy . . . you know the rest.

This is the same friend who tackled me with a hug one Christmas because I bought her brussels sprouts! I walked into a grocery store and saw those long stalks of brussels sprouts, and the thought occurred to me to put a big red bow on the top so it looked like a giant mistletoe and bring it to her desk at work. Her fiancé happened to be with her as she squealed in delight over this vegetable at her cubicle! Apparently, she had been craving them for dinner and had not seen any in the stores she had been shopping in. She was over the moon. Her fiancé came over that morning and said, "There was more excitement about the brussels sprouts than the ring I got her."

Kindness is following impulses that will cause no harm, are totally selfless, and sometimes seem like they make absolutely no sense. Learn to flow with thoughts like these so you can hear these seemingly out of the blue, spontaneous acts of kindness during a hurried and crazy time.

I have someone in my life who will deliver food to me at home or work without my asking. She knows how busy I am and that I might get so busy I do not make the time to eat (which is very unkind to my body, I know!). She does it without warning and often goes out of her way. Because of her taking heed of warm impulses to grab me dinner or lunch, it usually is right when I needed it.

Have you ever had someone on your heart and thought to call or email them? That person popping into your mind is a warm impulse that I suggest you start to listen to. So many times I have called someone I mentor, a friend, or someone I know in business and they say, "Wow, you called at the perfect time."

I am not suggesting there is science behind this; however, I am convinced, having been the recipient and the giver of spontaneous kindness, that it is almost instinctual. We can all sense or know a deeper connection with each other by following those warm and random impulses.

Kindness Gets You to Move

One Friday night in Manhattan I had an unexpected appointment on a subway train. It was raining and I wanted to stay inside. One of my mentees, Jasmine, invited me out. I had absolutely no desire to go. What got me to throw on a baseball cap over my dirty hair was that I had not seen this girl in several days. I thought it would be worth it just to be there for her. *Get it together, Adrienne,* I said to myself, knowing I needed to set an example that when you ask your mentor to be there for you, she cares enough to show up!

When I got to the train, there were delays. Arriving at the pitch-black auditorium to meet Jasmine, I found she was sitting in a group of about eight people. They were in the third balcony—the nosebleed section. The show wasn't exactly thrilling me. Immediately after, the whole group talked about getting food.

Surely I am here to help one of these guys, I thought. That is, I was there for my mentee—and open to anyone else I might help or encourage. Going out to eat is to me the "all-access pass" to break bread with a person you could be meant to meet. We began chatting about where we would go to grab dinner when I received a call from *my* mentor and separated from the group to answer.

We all need the kind of relationship in our lives—whether it's our kids, mom, or spouse—for whom it is a priority to make every effort to answer their call, even if you are out of the country or in a meeting. There's something powerful about making time for those calls. It causes you to value the relationship and your connection to them more. Taking those calls is what keeps me service minded. When you make kindness to those you honor and love a priority, no matter what you are in the middle of, it keeps you more in tune to the spontaneous acts of kindness we've discussed and in step with where you need to be in the moment. How you do one thing is what creates habits in all other areas. When I decide to make at least one person in my life a voice I will not deny, then I will be more in tune to hear the warm impulses, the voice of my own conscience, or that feeling that something or someone is not right for me, even within a crowd.

When there is chaos at home, an inundation of work on your desk, or thoughts of negativity and oppression in your mind, it is a time you need to hear someone's advice or wisdom more than ever. That's when you need to stop to respond to the small voice of a child who desperately needs time with you. It will help you to have peace about what you need to do as you make a big decision at a major crossroads in your life. Ultimately, *you need to know* that you are making the right decision. When you practice being open to that call from a special someone at any time, you are being intentional about tuning into the voices of people who are all around you—staff, administrators, legal counsel, customers—whose voices could easily be drowned out when you are busy juggling a hundred things. I have taken my mentor's calls on live television when he just happened to call as we were going to commercial break. I have picked up the phone while in a meeting with senior vice presidents of major corporations, and even in an interview once. No one asked me to do this; it is

WHEN I DECIDE TO MAKE AT LEAST ONE PERSON IN MY LIFE A VOICE I WILL NOT DENY, THEN I WILL BE MORE IN TUNE TO HEAR THE WARM IMPULSES, AND THE VOICE OF MY OWN CONSCIENCE.

a decision I made. Decide on a VIP—one who delivers the most peace and wisdom and who is an ally when the world is unkind and topsy-turvy.

Being on the phone with my mentor that night kept me at the venue. I told the group to go ahead of me. After I finished my call, I headed out to meet them . . . but one thing after another happened, and I started to feel like it was not meant to be. We all have moments in our lives when a situation just does not seem to be flowing or going as smoothly as it should be. We notice it most when we are doing something that should be relatively harmless (like getting tacos on a Sunday night!). My phone GPS was even acting up after I got off the train. I felt very turned around, even though I had been to the restaurant before. I could not seem to find the place, and my mentee and her friends, already there, were no help in giving directions. Neither were the three different people I stopped on the street to ask for help. By that time, I was getting frustrated.

I decided to stop and breathe. We've all heard stories of people getting a sixth sense awareness during times of danger. Through studying kindness firsthand, I have seen that when you are willing to be a helper or encourager, a kind of intuition kicks in for knowing where you need to be. You are not even thinking about it—you just know. As soon as I accepted that it was not happening for me to connect with this group of people, I headed home. It gave me time to make calls—one to another young woman I mentor in California, who I was able to encourage as I walked to another train stop on the way.

I spoke to my mentee for over thirty minutes walking through Manhattan, which put me near the 34th Street station. I decided to board there, even though it wasn't my usual way home. When I got on the subway, there were some passengers on board causing a scene. I made eye contact and smiled at a young woman sitting across from me because I could tell she was thinking the same thing I was. There is something hospitable about just acknowledging when life gets interesting! By the time my stop rolled around, I felt in my gut that I was supposed to introduce myself to her. I smiled again and said, "Hi, here's my card; you seem like a good person. Call if you need anything."

Two days later, I received this email at work:

> Hi Adrienne!
>
> This is the girl from the train Friday night (my name is Rebecca)! It was so nice to meet you briefly! That train ride was one of those odd New York City moments where you look around and have to find another normal stranger to share the moment with—haha! Anyway, thanks for giving me your card—I personally believe in divine moments like that where you feel moved to make a connection with someone, so thanks for reaching out. I was also surprised to discover that we both work in news—I would love to learn about what you do since I'm early in my career!
>
> Rebecca

The timing of our being on the same train at the same time could only happen because I was willing to go to dinner, then changed my plan, then went a different way home—as I was using kindness as my guide along the way. It also required me to see her as more than a face in the crowd.

Rebecca and I did meet in person after that train ride for some career and sisterly advice. It is interesting to me that we are conditioned to think it's okay to stop and ask someone attractive for their phone number to go on a date, or to even more casually hook up over an impressive bio and profile picture online, but then we will hesitate to be friendly or to connect with someone, not in a romantic sense, but in a "you sure look like someone who would be a good friend!" kind of way. If it works for something as primal as sexual attraction, why would it *not* work for a platonic relationship? Many women I know find it awkward, difficult, or nearly impossible to make new friends in big cities like LA or New York. I've endeavored to be friendly to people in large part because of that reason: people need people and the grind can be lonely. Yet there are great men and women all around us all the time waiting to meet others cut from the same cloth. It's okay to follow the impulse when you notice someone and think to yourself, *They look like a really good person.* Follow that and see if it leads to someone who could be a great addition to your tribe.

Finding the Right People

When I have gone the extra mile in my life, I've often ended up being pleasantly surprised by how it pays off. I had advertised on social media that I was looking for people who wanted mentoring and personalized coaching. This is, in and of itself, going the extra mile. It takes time, commitment, and energy when you choose to invest in the future of another; reciprocity would require people to invest in you in return.

I had set a deadline for people to turn in their applications. One of the young women contacted me *past the due date.* This sent a signal to me that she did not care whether she received the opportunity or not. Additionally, I was doing my best to create boundaries and value my time as I began mentoring more people. Yet something told me to give her a chance in spite of my rules. That gut instinct was confirmed when I looked over the message she sent me through her online profile, which was intriguing. When I finally gave her a call, in the middle of the conversation I said, "You are very gifted, though you don't even realize it. Let's set up a time to meet."

I arranged to have a face-to-face over lunch with her in my neighborhood. Bianca arrived on time, carrying a thank-you card and a box of cookies as a gift to me. She seemed nervous as I ate my salad while asking about her family and long-term goals. I decided that day that she could help me keep in touch with all the other young professionals I was mentoring. She jumped right on it and was always ready with a suggestion and reminders about what was on my calendar. Within weeks she was offering to order my groceries for delivery, run errands, and decorate my office without my asking. Within months she had become a partner and friend, and I welcomed her on as a member of my team. Had I not decided to make an exception for her, I would not have met this precious person in my life. Since I have known her, she has epitomized going the extra mile. Often you will have to go beyond what is typical to find what is exceptional.

Be Kind Even When You Don't Have to Be

In 2017 the stars aligned so I could meet a young reporter who needed some direction in his life and career. This was the year I was covering a total solar eclipse for ABC News, a huge story with over half a dozen reporters posted across the United States for an eclipse seen coast to coast. It was a one hundred–year event.

Matthew had contacted me over direct message on Instagram and excitedly given me some information about the town we were headed to. With deadlines and a large team of producers who were familiar with the area, I could have simply been *nice* and sent him a thank-you without reading his note. Instead I forwarded it to my producers. I sent him another DM so we could meet in person. What stood out was how polite and enthusiastic he was. Afterward he thanked me for making time for him and asked if I knew any voice coaches. I had already sensed that my greater purpose for traveling for work was to meet and help Matthew, so I typed back: "I suggest me."

He agreed. What he didn't bargain for is that I would help him *find his voice.* Over the course of a year I consulted him—more on having confidence in what he was saying than vocal quality. His biggest breakthrough came when I coached him on how to go the extra mile. I suggested he have coffee with city council members, CEOs, and other community leaders to get to know them. This would be an investment in the town, too, while allowing the movers and shakers to get to know him. I showed him that if they could trust him and knew he was invested, they would tell him their stories. I asked him to set a goal of doing this once every week or two. That effort led to major stories and opportunities other reporters in his market did not have. I taught him to care more about people than sounding or looking credible; it paid off in people allowing him to share those stories with an audience.

Early on I'd asked him why he wanted to do news. His response? "The news is a platform for people to trust you. We should want people to trust us." And he finally did see, a little over a year after we met, that *trust* was the voice I was coaching him to develop. Matthew wrote:

> I didn't realize it until this summer that all those things you were telling me, like going out and connecting with people over coffee, was for a bigger plan to really fall in love with this place. Now I'm truly connected and I'm going to be sad when I go.

Reflection: No One Just Arrives

Many times, people do not know what the ingredients are to success, even after they hear someone's story. A big factor in all of us being in the right place at the right time involves others being kind to us. We can think it's because we are talented or charming or because of our education but really, it's someone deciding to give us a shot. Then, at one point or another you become the game changer and deal maker! Follow your heart and kindness and you could be moved into position to make someone's day.

Who are your VIPs? Choose one or two voices you will not deny. If they call, you'll answer. These are examples of people you may want to prioritize connection to:

- Husband or wife
- Children
- Mentor
- Sister
- Business partner
- Agent

The last time you were in the right place at the right time, what led up to that moment? Who opened doors for you? How were you prepared, counseled, or trained with what seemed like spontaneous kindness?

Reflect on how it did not just happen, but that it was, instead, a series of steps and direction led with kind help that you could not have purposefully planned.

CHAPTER 12

FAVORITE THINGS: PAYING ATTENTION

Sentiment is so much of what drives us. A kind memory can fuel us to keep going in tough times.

One of the greatest ways to tap into kindness is to care about the things others care about. When you show this kind of consideration and attention to detail, you are empowered to connect in a special way with those close to you as well as strangers. You will be indelibly imprinted in their memory as a kind person.

Everyone has their special something that makes them smile. It could be the classic car in their driveway. For others, it's their favorite sports team or travel destination. The first thing is to connect through conversation. It does not cost you any money to pay attention to people when they talk about their motorcycle or their favorite restaurant.

The other day, I brought up my cameraman's boat and asked about the restoration he was working on. Rather than just ask how someone is today, remember those things that are important to them. It will be a much more interesting conversation for both of you, and these specifics prompt unexpected connections. It is helpful to research, ask about, and catalog those favorite things that will demonstrate caring consideration and honor. Extend this interest to family, professional connections, or those you meet and work with in the community. As far as shopping goes, I like to receive gifts that are specific and hand-selected for me, so I pay extra attention to what people say and what they like. I love to surprise them with something that is their favorite color or style or flavor, as if it was tailored for them! We can do things that seem small but are a big deal to those around us. It isn't necessarily about how much money was spent; a kind thought, action, and time makes it extremely valuable. I pay extra close attention when people are willing to go out of their way to make people feel treasured. Sometimes that requires a treasure hunt.

Lost and Found

I had traveled from frigid New York City to sunny Orlando wearing my new favorite coat that I had purchased just a couple of months earlier. While on vacation, I was called by ABC to travel south for an assignment three hours away in Fort Lauderdale. Packing up everything in my rental car, I knew I would not need my coat again until I was back in New York. After two weeks in Florida, my mission complete, I folded the jacket up and placed it on top of my straw beach tote and headed to the airport. A friend's husband was at the same airport at the same time, and we took the opportunity to catch up just outside the TSA checkpoint. I made the mistake of going through the standard line instead of PreCheck, then to the gate with my overstuffed carry-on bags. Breathing a sigh of relief, I reclined in my seat, thankful it was time to head home.

Forty minutes before landing I started to get a sinking feeling. As I reached up to get my bags from the overhead bin, I realized I didn't have my coat. I started panicking. I thought about how long it had taken me to find a coat I liked. Then I thought about how cold I would be dressed in resort clothing in New York in February. I checked under the seat. After deplaning I asked the gate agent if I could wait to make sure no other passenger had grabbed it by accident. Sadly, no coat. I called the airport lost-and-found department at JFK and then called TSA in Florida. I even took an extra hour as a crew member searched for the coat onboard one more time. Nothing.

I started to question my every move leading up to my getting on the flight. I had stopped to mail a friend's birthday present. Then I thought about how when I arrived at the airport, I was focused on chatting with my friend's husband. *Was I wrong for taking the time to do these things? Did an act of kindness cost me?* I wondered. *Was the coat lost because I was distracted by thinking about what I was supposed to be doing to reach out to other people?* I second-guessed everything I had done leading up to the lost coat. A successful trip seemed to be ending on a sour note.

Remember, when you are kind, events will sometimes challenge you to question whether your kindness is worth it. Shut those negative thoughts down!

I called lost-and-found again. Still no coat. A full week later I reached out to my field producer who had worked with me in Florida and who was still on the scene working with other reporters. I caught her on the day she was flying home. I had texted her a photo of my coat earlier in the week, hopeful it might turn up somewhere.

I asked if there was any way she could go by the lost-and-found when she arrived at the airport. She was happy to do it. The timing of this story is my favorite part. At the exact moment she arrived at the airport, the lost-and-found agents had just found my coat! I was walking in Manhattan when I received the notice by email, and I started jumping up and down. I had been making every effort to communicate with my producer. I didn't know she was standing at the lost-and-found counter *at the exact same time*, picking up the coat in person because she was able to provide the photo I'd texted her earlier! There was no hassle, no waiting, and she just picked it up as if we'd planned it and headed for her gate. She then texted me a note:

Your coat will soon be on its way!

She mailed it from our offices in Atlanta at no cost to me. I sent her an ecstatic text back:

THANK YOU!! YOU ARE AN ANGEL.

Maybe it sounds silly, but it is evident that I liked this coat! Think about your own special thing: your laptop, jewelry, or anything you would search for like a pot of gold! Everything was out of my control. Kindness is what will keep you from giving up hope when you can do nothing to change a situation. Don't just depend on what you can control. Depend on kindness to help you.

The Shirt Off Your Back

I have fun telling this story involving another one of my favorite things: an amazing sweater that looked like it cost hundreds, though I paid far less. Everywhere I went I received compliments when I wore this sweater. Strangers, coworkers, and a couple of the hair and makeup artists had asked me where to buy it.

I decided since people liked it so much, I would go back to the store and pick up several and bring them in for those who had asked what store carried the sweaters. Two of the staff paid me for them and were thrilled to get such an amazing deal. There was one woman, though, who surprised me. She was part of our crew and more than twice my age. She had complimented the sweater and exclaimed, "That would look good on me!" Her boldness made me laugh inside, but while picking up those extra sweaters I decided I would pay for hers and gift it to her the next time I came in for work.

DON'T JUST DEPEND ON WHAT YOU CAN CONTROL. DEPEND ON KINDNESS.

When I handed her the bag, she peeked inside and shouted, "Really? Wow. Thank you so much, Adrienne." She was visibly moved. She threw the sweater on over her clothes and in a childlike way popped into the area I was getting ready in, saying, "Look! It fits!"

She later wrote me the sweetest card on beautiful stationery and let me know that she had been working two jobs and her husband was working and they hadn't had a chance to celebrate her birthday. "This is my birthday sweater," she wrote, scribbling a doodle of herself in the sweater inside the card.

It is always nice when people appreciate and receive the gifts you bring. I can recall working in local news and having viewers contact me, wanting to bring me things they thought would complement me or my wardrobe.

There was the one viewer whose mother had passed away. She brought me all kinds of costume jewelry simply because she enjoyed watching me on the news. At first, I didn't know how to receive this gift, yet I knew I shouldn't refuse the gift of her mother's heirlooms to me. There was this gentleman who came down with his wife, and he had handmade me a few pairs of earrings, including a note that he would repair them if needed. I still have a card that he wrote, telling me about his creations. My first-grade teacher gifted me jewelry made from antique African beads every year as a thank-you for reading to the children at the elementary school I attended for Read Across America Day. Another one of my recent stories is that of our ninety-one-year-old wardrobe stylist, Joe. He has been working his whole life, and he always notices little things. He made a pair of earrings and brought them in for me to wear. On my birthday, he was thoughtful enough to make me a card and a beaded necklace.

Giving and showing appreciation for these gifts is so important. It's our way of showing each other that we are all important and contributing.

Over the holidays one year I had to travel internationally, and for some reason it was very important for me to send out cards to a select group of people. It was only an hour before my flight, I needed to return my rental car, and I was twenty minutes away. I stopped by a friend's home to see if she wouldn't mind dropping off some of the cards.

"I can take them all and deliver your mom's card tomorrow, just in time for the holiday."

I was very grateful. There were times that I could tell my being away was not my mother's favorite thing, but when I received her text, I knew that she appreciated the gesture.

"Thank you for the sentiment in the card," it read.

I have found many people love a handwritten card or some quality time. That is what means the world to them. One of the young women I mentor will pick me up whenever I fly to Dallas. She is happy to do it because I would be getting a car service. This way, she can have some good time and conversation with someone she cares about. It would cost me thirty or forty dollars to pay for a ride to my hotel; instead I am able to invest in someone and she is able to invest in me by an act of kindness.

Phone calls are another one of my favorite things. When someone calls and you are off doing something spectacular, you can share the excitement. Maybe you just wish you had someone to share your good news, feelings, or hardships with, and you can't do it in person. Hearing that person's voice on the other end of the phone is one of the best feelings in the world and affirms that you are loved. With video calling provided now in so many different ways, it almost feels like your loved ones are with you.

I have a favorite restaurant in Folsom, California. It might just be one of the greatest Thai restaurants in the world. Any time I call, the owners and staff make sure that I can get a good seat, prepare their specialties, and treat me and my friends like rock stars. The location is about forty minutes away from any one of the people I am visiting, so they know we will be in the car together for a long time. It is absolutely a labor of love to have anyone join me because it is so far out of the way. Believe me, it is worth the drive. Kindness is getting stuck with me on the way to my favorite restaurant!

Go the Extra Mile

To "go the extra mile" is what we all need to do and use as a mantra to be fully engaged in life. There is a reward attached to special effort to reach a goal or make an impact. Bonus: you are already going to great lengths in any area where you have a favorite thing or are a passionate fan. You might also be going the extra mile in any area where you feel it will benefit the bottom line; we all want to do things we think will pay off for us now or later.

I have seen throughout my professional career times when teams made an extra effort to impress their boss or a client. I watched people turn on and off that charm, and I made a deliberate choice that I would get to the place in life in which I was the same with everyone I met, everywhere I went. If I was going to be charming, it would be 24/7 so I never was caught out of character. As a young professional, I realized no one can maintain a persona they have to fake for too long. Kindness is a force that allows you to be passionate and positive and make people feel amazing, without exaggeration. Kindness gives you the power to go to great lengths without trying too hard.

KINDNESS DOES NOT BREAK THE RULES, IT EXPANDS THE IMAGINATION.

I'll never forget a story from a man twice my age describing his father, who worked for an automaker in the 1950s. Every time the office phone rang, his father answered it like it was the president of the company calling. It did not matter if he was expecting a call from the facilities manager or a secretary; he addressed everyone with the utmost respect. Kindness treats everyone from the janitor to the stranger on the street to the celebrity, the executive, even your family, like they are worth your going the extra mile.

Choosing to go the extra mile requires listening intently. One of my managers complimented a blouse I was wearing. Since she liked it so much, I contacted the company and ordered it in what I hoped was her size. I do not know that people would think to buy a manager clothing, but I took time out of my day to make that call like I would for my mom or sister, and it fit perfectly.

In Texas, I was friends with a woman who had an exchange student from South Korea staying with her family. This student's dream was to be a flight attendant, and one of our mutual friends had rented this girl a flight attendant costume! This got my wheels turning. I called up a major airline and asked if they would allow this young lady to come and take photos inside the plane as part of a vision board. The airline ended up going the extra mile and giving us a personal tour of the crew training facility. We shot the whole experience on my iPhone, and my producer was kind enough to put it on our newscast! We sent a DVD of the story to her mother in Seoul. Kindness does not break the rules, it expands the imagination.

We all want to be ready in life to do something extra special. *Extra* can be used as slang to describe someone being over the top, dramatic. It is often used positively, to describe larger-than-life personalities, interests, and behavior. This is a clue for what our purpose should be! *You can never have too much kindness. Be extra.*

Reflection Time

What are some of your favorite things or memories? Send a letter to those who have helped you, thanking them for kindnesses they have shown in small ways that were major for you. Then think of some of your favorite people's favorite things. Can you make their day extra special with something simple? Here are some ideas to jumpstart you:

- Paint an inspiring image that would speak to them.
- Personally craft a version of a vision board for them based on things you know are on their dream list.
- Write them a poem.
- Offer to babysit or mow their lawn.
- If you need to budget for a larger item—save up money every week, even if it requires cutting back for a bit. Consider gifts that will last, like a monthly subscription or delivery service.

Creativity is birthed by necessity without thinking about what you can afford. Do not take on any pressure of paying for it. Think about it: when you were a kid, you did not concern yourself with how much things cost. You just wanted that Lamborghini or new sneakers. You just dreamed. Use your imagination and think of some fun and exciting things you could do for a friend, boss, or mentor that revolve around their favorite things, without giving a thought to the cost. Dream like the idea is your own:

- Ask your manager's favorite airline if some of the staff could wish your boss a happy birthday on video.
- Call and ask a company to honor your mentor with a "key to the city" style promotion so they receive a discount or free goodies.
- Get a book or magazine subscription to help your friend or boss with a goal they have been talking about—for example, investing, home decorating, or fitness.

- Make it a habit to gather a fun personal fact on the people you meet. For example, I found out the former president of Disney World's favorite character is Eeyore. You can save a note like this in your contacts as a reminder when it is time to send a card or gift.

CHAPTER 13

THE POWER OF GIVING

When you give your time and assets for others, you receive a special delivery of what can be surprising and priceless results.

Generosity is one of the most vital displays of being who we really are and developing an identity rooted in kindness. This final chapter highlights the total paradigm shift required to live out kindness in action.

Living a life of kind giving means looking at your resources and the resources of others to become more creative. When we are having our toughest moments in life, getting refocused on giving can be a huge inspiration to renew passion. When we give more, we live more. We live more purposed and productive lives, which will allow us to be truly present as we work, play, and go on this journey to ultimate fulfillment.

In order to truly possess this kind of openness, we must think of ourselves making a bigger mark on the world—one that will affect neighborhoods, families, and generations beyond our own. In order to do that, you have to think like a person who has a wealth of resources, which could mean cash, friends, connections, business associates, and talents. This is why: if you think of yourself as not having enough, as someone who is lacking in gifts, talents, friends, or connections, you may prevent yourself from stepping out and being generous. You will be, or likely have been, more concerned about your own needs, like paying your bills, than being benevolent. Your money situation can change. What should not change is your kindness; you should remain constant and current in that. Being current in kindness becomes your *currency*, and generosity is an outpouring of that.

Kindness Is Your Currency

As fast paced as our schedules and the world we live in can be, we need to initiate a new way of not getting left behind. Like technology that is constantly changing, there are more demands on us to be nimble and quick. I think of the hand-eye coordination it takes to execute specific moves in a video game. There are seemingly endless plays in our routine, jobs, and relationships, as well as surprises in our daily life that could throw us off course. Staying in a kind zone, where we might stop to assist someone when it was not in our original plan, hones our ability to turn on a dime and be ready at a moment's notice.

> **Currency**, *noun*
> The state of being commonly known or accepted, or of being used in many places[14]

Kindness should be our commonly accepted behavior and motive. Kindness also keeps you current and present rather than simply going through the motions or being stuck in survival mode.

When all we can think about is survival, we are less inclined to be kind. I was talking to a young lady who is a reporter and news anchor in a small town. Being from a major city, she was having a hard time adjusting and felt that the very tight-knit community was excluding her. She came in with some excitement about pursuing her dream, but soon she began to complain and gossip. Her attitude had soured about the career path she was on and she felt she had plateaued.

WHEN ALL WE CAN THINK ABOUT IS SURVIVAL, WE ARE LESS INCLINED TO BE KIND.

I first asked her what her dream was. She explained to me that it was to have a family, be financially more comfortable than her parents, and make a difference for people. I told her that even though she wanted to help people, that desire was being eclipsed by the pressure she felt to make good money. She did not have the same passion because she was in survival mode. She had the same capacity to be kind but was not using that muscle because she was only going through the motions as she waited for her contract to be over. She was forgetting that her purpose at work was not just to do a great job on camera, but to make a difference in the lives of those she came in contact with.

When we notice ourselves in survival mode, we have unknowingly become depleted. Whether by the trials of life, overworking ourselves, or a lack of rest, we have lost power. We've all had our cell phone in the red zone with less than 20 percent battery life left. When you see your phone is nearly out of juice and you don't have a way to charge it immediately, you'll hesitate to use it in order to preserve the battery. You'll avoid using it for its everyday functions; you will not text or make calls unless you absolutely have to . . . until you can get to a place where you can *recharge.* In life, if we feel overtaxed or that life has demanded too much of us, we start to pull back and act more reserved. We will stop doing the things we were made for, that we are equipped for, all because we are in self-preservation mode. This is why we need to stay charged, because we don't want to pull back from living generously and confidently, which is the essence of who we really are. Kindness recharges your battery, even when you think you've got nothing left.

Getting out of survival mode will take a moment. You need to stop and replace the thoughts that you are in need, or have lack in your life, or are somehow limited to attaining the answers you are seeking. Instead you need to decide you are so grateful that *you have answers for someone else.* Remember, when you are helping someone, you are less likely to consider your own needs and challenges. You are just doing the right thing, kindly and selflessly.

The same approach can be used at any time of your life. This is where imagination is truly useful: Take a breath and imagine that all your needs are met and money is no object. Imagine that time is not an issue and you are not delayed or late in life. The key is to meditate on what you need to do next, no matter your circumstances or pressures in life. One way you can do that is to ask yourself, *What would someone rich and famous do in this situation?* The reason I use this question is that it helps when meditating on having zero financial limitations. The pressure of how much something costs does not come into a wealthy person's mind; they have the liberty to spend or give what they want. I want you to have that same liberty (and you can), which will allow you to be more creative. Here are the thoughts that pop in my mind after much practice in asking the question myself:

- **CALL A FRIEND.** Wealthy and famous people are constantly calling in favors. They *know people who know people* for their connections. They don't have to do it alone when it comes to giving and helping others.
- **TAKE TIME TO CONSIDER AND THINK OF IDEAS.** Famous people are big thinkers and doers. They will strategize and plan for what they want to do and how best to achieve it.
- **DELIVERY.** Famous people are usually rich in money and short on time, so they get things shipped or delivered by courier. Transportation is often one half of a very big gift to an organization or charity.

Think outside the box right now. You have friends who work for companies that are generous. Around the holidays many have money earmarked for charity or are looking for ways to be more of a help to organizations and communities. One of the kindest things you can do is help others know where it is best to give; they are looking for who can take dollars and turn them into impact. Sometimes people and companies will spontaneously give because they hear the passion from someone endorsing an organization, and it becomes contagious. While working on a business deal, a friend of mine in sales secured a donation for 1,500 pairs of socks in New York for a hospital on the West Coast! That is amazing! Of course, she had other business to do, but she was willing to think of others and conveyed kindness in her few conversations with the client.

I was part of a nonprofit cause one year and found out that a charitable foundation in the same state had been giving away cash donations in their city. I sent the information to the contact I had worked with, and later learned it paid off—with a check! I didn't have to fundraise or ask for the money myself, all I had to do was think of others. Here is the letter I was sent in response:

> Hi Adrienne,
>
> I hope this finds you well. Regarding the information you sent about the foundation, as it turns out, we've been able to cultivate a wonderful relationship with them, and they recently granted us $10,000 to support the work of our juvenile intervention programs for adjudicated and at-risk youth. Thank you for thinking of us and forwarding this information.
>
> With gratitude for all you do, RD

I am sharing this story to inspire you and to show you that you don't have to have millions or even thousands of dollars in order to make a difference. You can have a thousand-dollar or million-dollar idea! Creativity empowers you to think more innovatively.

In another instance, I emceed an event for an organization that helps at-risk youth. I wanted to help them in some way beyond my appearance that evening. I had visited the youth center and was informed that most of them had dressed up for the cameras, but in fact they had little else in the way of nice clothes or shoes besides what they had worn that day. (It is important that when you give, you involve others who know and appreciate the joy of giving.) I was in the middle of a conference when I was reminded to send some clothing to this organization. I sent a message to a friend who works for a major athletic corporation:

> Hey lady! Think you can help me send some T-shirts to a youth group?

Within an hour I received a yes and the package was in the mail. I sent the email to the woman at the organization, letting her know to expect it. Just like the $10,000 check I didn't write, I didn't buy the shirts. Yet kindness gets creative when it comes to giving and remembering what other people are working on to help the community.

One year I hosted an event for single women on Valentine's Day—the only problem is I had decided to host this party with only three weeks to plan! I was determined to do something special in spite of the timeline, so I started calling everyone I could think of. A restaurant manager friend of mine delivered a huge ice chest I could use for the drinks and ice cream, and a few of the young women I mentored were volunteering to help me set up. I had reached out to one of my colleagues who works with several beauty and fashion brands for ideas about items I could include in a swag bag. She messaged me back immediately, unbothered by my last-minute request. All she wanted to know was how many people I was expecting. Not only did she provide gifts for 100 people at no charge to me, she had them delivered to my apartment by courier within a day or two! The day before the party I realized I hadn't picked up bags to put the goodies in! Then I remembered that the man who helped me find my last apartment happened to own a company that manufactured gift bags! His wife dropped them off the day of and we were able to surprise women with beautiful items on a holiday that can be really lonely. I believe they left feeling the love!

At ABC News, one of the hairstylists, Petula Skeete, had a few passion projects involving working with youth. One day she told me about how she was paying out of her own pocket for a three-course meal in order to teach a group of boys at a halfway home about etiquette. I was touched by her story of a child who was frustrated by all the nice food and the lessons on table manners. Petula needed to know why he kept acting out, throwing a fit. She took the time to talk things out with him and found out that he really liked peanut butter and jelly sandwiches. She asked him, "If I buy you a loaf of bread and a whole jar of peanut butter and your own jar of jelly, will you participate in the etiquette course?"

Petula said this young man not only agreed to be involved in the program, but she witnessed a dramatic change in his mood. As much as I enjoyed the story, I quickly thought of the fact that she was funding this out of her own pocket. I looked at her and said: "Listen, you don't ever have to buy food again. You need to talk to restaurants. Create a proposal for what kind of food you're looking for, or for the groceries to make the meal, then make sure to video record the whole meal and the boys enjoying their food. There are so many places in New York that are willing to help charitable causes like yours. I totally support you in this."

She looked surprised and then agreed that she would do it. Days later she reached out to a local chain restaurant and they agreed to partner with her. We were chatting several weeks after that conversation and she said, "Adrienne, I want you to know that thanks to *you* we are fully sponsored for our event. The restaurant is going to provide meals for my December program."

I tell you this story to help you see what you are capable of. I did not underwrite the event or wash dishes or serve any of these kids, yet I still was a big part of this plan to give. This is what you are able to do too—by developing and being open to the art of kindness, you can listen and lend your ideas and creativity to bring results. Kindness is your currency! Simply be yourself and give of yourself. Giving thoughtfulness to someone who is striving to be generous confirms to them that their purpose matters, their diligence matters, and they are on the right path.

Thoughtfulness Refreshes

Another woman I have befriended directs PR for a clothing line and wanted to have a fashion show. She was discouraged by the overwhelming load of work she was under to put this event together. Her mother was having health issues, which caused her some worry as well.

"Maybe," I said, "this need your mother has is your ticket to some much-needed rest. See it as a gift in disguise. Schedule your vacation so that you're not only doing the caretaker role. Take time to dream and script out your event. You have to promise me that you will take time every day to get quiet."

THE PURPOSE OF GIVING . . . IS TO ERADICATE A SENSE OF LACK IN YOU, SO YOU TRULY UNDERSTAND NOTHING IS IMPOSSIBLE.

She agreed and went away for five days of peace. She came back rejuvenated and with greater clarity about what she wanted to do for this event. I encouraged her to ask friends to provide services like hair and makeup and reach out to anyone she already knew in the industry who would be willing to do her a favor. Before long, others had agreed to provide a location and food. I could not make the event myself; however, I contacted some of the young women I knew and asked if they would be willing to volunteer to help her with whatever she needed. Two of them stepped up. Remarkably, when her makeup artist showed up sick for the night, it was one of my girls—who had gone to cosmetology school—who ended up being the replacement! Just having someone to tell her the event was a great idea and then give her the wisdom she needed to set herself apart to clear her head was the step that set her in the right direction.

Do not ever think that because you don't give millions of dollars to charitable causes that your giving is small. Giving is ultimately priceless, because you cannot put a dollar amount on a kind act, an outstretched hand, or the right word at just the right time. As these examples demonstrate, it is about doing whatever is needed at the time and being creative about how to be a solution for others. The purpose of giving is not to just have the power to transfer funds, it is to eradicate a sense of lack in you, so you truly understand nothing is impossible and realize your capacity for being absolutely limitless in your imagination and expectations. With every generous act, large or small, we are shaping and building a legacy.

Give Yourself a Fighting Chance

The only thing that can truly create in us the level of fulfillment that I call the sweet spot—that place of having your cake and eating it too—is attitude. That attitude is a direct reflection of our identity rooted in kindness. Deciding to be kind to someone, whether they are pleasant to us or not, is the difference between a good day and a bad day. In a world that is always changing, we have to be willing to say, "I am kind!" before we fight to say, "I am right and you are wrong!" Winning an argument may seem justified, yet it cannot bring fulfilment.

I had to come to this conclusion recently: I will not make tension in a relationship or a debate over the direction of a project at work my deal breakers. My attitude is the most precious possession I own because it is linked to the real me—the kind me. If my attitude begins to change, it means I need to go back to a picture of who I really am. I encourage you to keep a trigger word in your purse or briefcase bag or as a screensaver on your phone. What is the trigger that will remind you that an argument or, for example, giving in to the rudeness of a stranger in line at the airport, is not worth it? Make a list to describe who you really are (or the person you intend to be). Here is a sample list:

- I think of others first.
- I am always calm.
- I am willing to change my perspective.
- I am eager to be the bigger person.
- Kindness is my superpower.

Remember, kindness has the ability to satisfy us like nothing else. Most of us learn over time (and sometimes the hard way) that nothing we can buy will ever fill our hearts. The best job, or having more money, or even a relationship with another person will never completely satisfy us. Recognizing your identity as a kind person is the biggest gift we can give ourselves. Your inherent gifts and talents—as well as abilities you have not even known you have deep within you—will be drawn out as you are kind. Kindness demonstrates your significance and settles you when you do not know what to do next. It is imperative that you see what a difference you're

KINDNESS SETTLES YOU WHEN YOU DO NOT KNOW WHAT TO DO NEXT.

making. From career to connection, I want kindness to be the center of every prescription, every invoice, and every contract. This makes me unstoppable because no one can duplicate who I am, and no matter what job or task I am given, I will find purpose and meaning.

Genuine Interest

Another reason kindness is a superpower is that it gives what looks like the mundane or inconsequential a shot at being meaningful. I've already shared how whenever I am on assignment, I am keenly aware of the job that I am being paid to do, and I am always willing for there to be another reason or purpose for that assignment. It may be a meaningful conversation you have with a colleague or client while on the job. The key is to avoid assumptions, stay open to the unexpected, and allow other opportunities to flow while you are focused on the task at hand.

One evening, we were doing a story for *World News Tonight*. There was a struggle in getting new information and, down to the wire, we ran into roadblocks. Police were still looking for witnesses and possible suspects. We thought we had video of the victim, a young man with autism, speaking out. However, it turned out to be the wrong victim. The story was worth telling, but we were stressed with deadlines, and since we will only report what we can confirm with law enforcement, it ended up being a very short story on air. After the show, I sat down on a couch in an empty waiting room, wondering if the stress was worth it and if we had done the story justice. I closed my eyes and took a deep breath. "I am doing this story for a reason. Why are we really doing it?" I whispered.

Minutes later, I received an email about our piece from a producer in New York. She had not worked on the story; she was simply watching from another editing booth. Her note read:

> Subject: Thank you for your story tonight
>
> That happened in the town I grew up in and my whole community is outraged.
>
> My nephew has autism & my older brother was very grateful this got national attention.
>
> Thanks again.
>
> Xoxo K

I sat up in my chair and was so grateful for her note. If you slow down and breathe, you will see that when you are doing what is asked of you and what needs to be done, you are not working in vain. Everything—even the steps along the way that seem inconsequential—can teach you something and have a purpose. If you allow it, these moments will create in you a habit of taking ownership and giving your best, even when it looks like it is no big deal or a waste of time. When we decide to be kind, every minute of our lives can count for something, because there will be someone and something worth being fully engaged in wherever you are, whether millions are watching and cameras are rolling or not.

Love in Your Eyes

As you are kind and giving to others, the love you have for people is going to grow more and more. From my earliest days of college and then working in TV, I would not have heard anything about love in regard to journalism. I have never heard of a practical application of love in the television or business arena. Yet my mentor told me something I will never forget, and he repeated it many times over the course of the years I have known him: "Adrienne, when you look into that camera, I want love to come out of your eyes."

He was encouraging me to intentionally display warmth as I spoke to viewers and my co-anchors. Some people in television have told me that they look into the camera and imagine a loved one, like their grandmother or a friend, in order to connect through that lens. I don't see anyone in particular—I just see myself making intentional and caring eye contact with that person watching, wherever they are. For some it is difficult to fathom an audience that they cannot see. But it is needed more than ever in our world of interconnectedness with viewers, followers and, friends online who are as present as someone standing next to you. One of the greatest gifts you can give to someone is to truly see them, eye-to-eye, and this is true in person and on TV.

Another message I received from the documentary *Won't You Be My Neighbor?* was that children saw Fred Rogers as talking to them from inside the TV. The same is true of online channels and social media. It is possible to make a genuine, intimate connection with people through the lens, on stage, and within arm's reach. Displaying your true self through showing a kind interest in another human being provides a quick connection, even from a distance.

One of my favorite women to quote is Eleanor Roosevelt, who famously said, "One thing life has taught me: if you are interested, you never have to look for new interests. They come to you. . . . When you are genuinely interested in one thing, it will always lead to something else."[15] People feel seen and heard when we show interest in them and display a genuine interest in what matters to them. Reflect on the times you truly cared about how you responded to someone you could have simply passed by. Rehearse and repeat that eye-to-eye engagement. It leads to more interests and interesting conversations and opportunities that you could not have planned—not just for the people you already know and agree with but the people you meet at the holiday party or the friend of a friend.

All of the answers to your questions—and the great adventure you are looking for—will come as you take a genuine interest in people. You will be amazed by how kindness leads you to boldly discover more than you could have imagined. Being kind will turn everyday events into your most memorable experiences. Growth will come from seeing and knowing others with a desire to be a part of improving their lives, accepting them, and standing with them to see *their* doors open. The choice to be fully present and engaged will maximize your everyday enjoyment.

It is my intention each day that I give myself fully in every interaction, empowered to be the real me and honoring the time I have on this planet. That is what puts air in our lungs; it is what life feels like. No matter where we go and what we do, as we come to a greater knowledge of kindness, we will be supercharged to overcome any odds. No matter what comes against us, a true interest in people and in kindness will maintain our optimism with hope that any situation is subject to change. Through kindness, we have the power to be the change agents, trailblazers, and superheroes our world not only needs, but is asking for.

ACKNOWLEDGMENTS

Thanks to my mom and my dad and my entire family for being the reason this book was written. Thank you to all the friends, loved ones, and colleagues over many years for, in one way or another, teaching me humility; for the importance of a gentle response; and for telling me the truth to help me discover how to truly be myself.

SUGGESTED RESOURCES

Here is a list of organizations I have mentioned throughout the book or that I have worked with that you can partner with to display kindness to your community:

- LIGHT (Loving Individuals Giving Help Together) / Fort Worth, TX (and beyond)
- Sacramento Helping Hands / North Highlands, CA
- Family Learning Center / North Highlands, CA
- PEI Kids, Inc. / Trenton, NJ
- BeautyFULL / New York, NY
- Mercy San Juan Medical Center / Carmichael, CA
- Studio T Urban Dance Academy / Sacramento, CA

@5forsure

This is my daily inspiration through social media as we campaign to take five minutes to work on a goal, give a pep talk to a friend, or brainstorm a dream with a friend. I have learned that if you want an audience with anyone, especially a high-powered executive, do not ask for lunch or coffee! The key is to ask for five minutes. Take the @5forsure challenge on Instagram and make time to invest in yourself and others for five minutes a day. Taking five minutes every day is not only doable, it's also impactful.

Bill Krause Coaching

I've been consulted by this man for over a decade and can say I wouldn't be here without his highly specialized insights, course correction, and problem-solving skills. Frankly, I don't know how people make it when they don't have a business and life coach. We don't always know what is stopping us from going forward or from hitting our stride. Bill is my tour guide, and now I am sharing him with you. Log on to www.billkrausecoaching.com.

NOTES

1. *American Dictionary of the English Language*, s.v. "kind (*adj.*)," accessed December 31, 2019, http://webstersdictionary1828.com/Dictionary/kind.
2. *American Dictionary of the English Language*, s.v. "kind (*noun.*)," accessed December 31, 2019, http://webstersdictionary1828.com/Dictionary/kind.
3. Diane von Furstenberg, *The Woman I Wanted to Be* (2015; repr., New York: Simon & Schuster, 2014).
4. *Merriam-Webster*, s.v. "nice (*adj.*)," accessed December 31, 2019, https://www.merriam-webster.com/dictionary/nice.
5. Copyright, Kent M. Keith, 1968, renewed 2001.
6. Calvin Harris; Taylor Swift, *This Is What You Came For*, Westbury Road and Columbia Records, 2016.
7. *Merriam-Webster*, s.v. "capture lightning in a bottle (*idiom*)," accessed December 31, 2019, https://www.merriam-webster.com/dictionary/lightning%20in%20a%20bottle.
8. Neville, Morgan, dir. *Won't You Be My Neighbor?* (Los Angeles: Tremolo Productions, 2018)
9. *Lexico*, s.v. "reciprocity (*noun*)," accessed December 31, 2019, https://www.lexico.com/definition/reciprocity.

10. *American Dictionary of the English Language*, s.v. "interview (*noun*.)," accessed December 31, 2019 http://webstersdictionary1828.com/Dictionary/interview.
11. *Lexico*, s.v. "kind (*adj*.)," accessed December 31, 2019, https://www.lexico.com/definition/kind.
12. "Why Former U.S. Surgeon General Vivek Murthy Believes Loneliness Is a 'Profound' Public Health Issue" (video), *Washington Post*, May 15, 2018, https://www.washingtonpost.com/video/postlive/former-surgeon-general-dr-vivek-murthy-people-who-are-lonely-live-shorter-lives/2018/05/15/4632188e-5853-11e8-9889-07bcc1327f4b_video.html.
13. Ceylan Yeginsu, "U.K. Appoints a Minister for Loneliness," *New York Times*, January 17, 2018, https://www.nytimes.com/2018/01/17/world/europe/uk-britain-loneliness.html.
14. *American Dictionary of the English Language*, s.v. "currency (*noun*)," accessed December 31, 2019, http://webstersdictionary1828.com/Dictionary/currency.
15. Roosevelt, Eleanor. *You Learn By Living*. Harper & Row, 1960.

ABOUT THE AUTHOR

Adrienne Bankert is an Emmy and Edward R. Murrow Award–winning national correspondent and anchor for ABC News, *Good Morning America*, *World News Tonight*, and *Nightline*. She reported live from Chiang Rai, Thailand, during the rescue of thirteen boys and their soccer coach as the world watched the historic rescue. She traveled to London to cover the royal wedding of Prince Harry and Meghan Markle, and she was the first network journalist to report live from the scene when several police officers were massacred in Dallas, Texas, in 2016. Her compelling interviews with guests that range from wounded warriors to celebrities, including Lady Gaga, Bradley Cooper, Dwayne Johnson, Ryan Reynolds, and more, have gained widespread attention. She has worked in local news in Sacramento, Dallas–Fort Worth, and in Los Angeles as a host and anchor, as well as a health and wellness and general assignment reporter. She remains committed to the goal she declared early on in her journey to "change the face of television," and she is a regular speaker at events, providing practical and inspirational wisdom that launches people into the highest and best versions of their lives.

Adrienne is passionate about financial literacy and teaching generosity to all ages, having partnered with a number of charities. She is a philanthropic engineer, helping to architect new ways to meet needs and make dreams come true that are worthwhile investments for community and corporate partners.

As a consultant, Adrienne is a friend, mentor, and tour guide to men and women—from established industry leaders to those in the early stages of their career—helping them find their way in the greatest adventure they will ever embark upon: LIFE.